JOURNEY INTO THE DARK

ENNIO CONTINI

For my brother, Ralph, and my sister, Mary Ann,
and their families

—M. P.

CONTENTS

Preface

In 1952, Olivia Rossetti Agresti, a daughter of William Michael Rossetti who was then in her late seventies, was in the midst of a sporadic, decades-long correspondence with Ezra Pound. On August 10 of that year, she wrote to tell Pound that she had received a copy of a newly published volume called *L'alleluja*, whose cover proclaimed: *Poesie di Ennio Contini e Ezra Pound* (Pound's contribution consisted of the first ten of his Cantos in an Italian translation by his daughter, Mary de Rachewiltz, "*in collaborazione personale con l'Autore*"). In her letter, she took issue with the order of the names: "It shld surely be *Ezra Pound e Ennio Contini*; the one of world-wide reputation, the other so far a nonentity." In his reply on August 15, Pound addressed the point briefly but decisively: "No / I approve the order in Contini's vol."

He offered no explanation of his view, but it is possible to speculate on several factors that may have informed it. For one thing, throughout his life Pound was energetically generous in his assistance to and promotion of other writers whom he considered worthy. For another, Contini's contribution to the volume consisted of eleven original, previously unpublished poems, while Pound's was a translation, presented without the original texts, of material that had first appeared more than a quarter of a century earlier. Also, Contini, admittedly lacking a "world-wide reputation," had published essays in prominent Italian journals; his poetry had appeared in anthologies and a small collection, and had been translated into Greek; thus, in his own country (where the book had been published, after all), he was hardly the "nonentity" of Agresti's characterization. And although it may have seemed to her that Contini was piggybacking on the American poet's fame, Contini had originally, in a letter to Pound—who was then confined in St. Elizabeths Hospital in Washington, D.C.—proposed the joint publication as a first step in restoring Pound's poetic presence in Italy, where his work had fallen into neglect, a proposal that Pound had obviously accepted.

In the period of his correspondence with Pound and the publication of *L'alleluja*, Contini was himself under confinement, held in a series of prisons for actions relating to his service in the Italian army during the Second World War. In 1947, while in the prison on the island of Procida, off the coast of Naples, Contini met twenty-year-old Alfredo de Palchi, who was in the middle of his own six-year stint in various prisons (he had been convicted on completely fabricated political charges, of which he would be fully exonerated some years later). At least some of Contini's loneliness and isolation must have been eased by this encounter with a young man of similar sensibility and interests. De Palchi credits Contini with educating him about his earliest inspiration, Villon; introducing him to Kafka, Faulkner, and other modern writers; and encouraging his own first serious efforts at writing poetry.

After their release, de Palchi visited Contini twice, first in 1953 and then, more than fifty years later, in May 2006, six months before Contini's death (this meeting is described in detail in Luigi Fontanella's essay "Alfredo de Palchi: Between Essay and Hi(s)tory," on de Palchi's Web site). Throughout his life, de Palchi has continued to acknowledge his debt to the elder poet. In collections of poetry published in 1967 and 2006, he expressed his profound gratitude to Contini for having inspired him. When de Palchi was awarded the NOBELito ("little Nobel Prize") in 2008, the accompanying interview carried a dedication to "Ennio Contini poeta maestro amico." His ultimate homage to the man he calls his master is, of course, the present volume.

Most people would agree that these consistent expressions of gratitude are touching, even admirable, especially in an age when many seem to regard irony and cynicism as the only distinguishing marks of authenticity. But much more than a sense of obligation has impelled the commission and the publication of this translation. The publisher of Chelsea Editions has always valued artistic independence and integrity above all else, and this volume, like every preceding one in the series, has been motivated by the desire to acquaint English-speaking readers with the work of an Italian poet of genuine accomplishment. Contini is, admittedly, an uneven and sometimes difficult poet, and he is also a poet of considerable variety—so much so that it is difficult at times to form a coherent view of his sensibility and accomplishment. Who is the poet Ennio Contini? Is he the creator of charming evocations of sea and countryside, of tender celebrations of family love, of anguished cries torn from a caged and condemned soul, of hymns of hope of a better life to come? The obvious answer is that he is all of these, and more.

For all that we celebrate growth and variety as hallmarks of great writers, critical opinion tends to favor those who fence off their own acre and work it continually over those who restlessly seek fresh woods and pastures new—often to the extent that a bad book by a great writer will receive more attention than a good book by a good writer. In her comprehensive treatment of Contini's life and writings, Francesca Bergadano argues convincingly for an animating spirit of consistency throughout his career. Yet, at the same time, I value his work for the equally strong element of experiment and discovery that seems to me to underlie it.

My first interaction with that work came several years ago, when I decided to translate three of Contini's poems as my contribution to a book of tributes to Alfredo de Palchi. When I was later asked to undertake the present translation, I accepted, frankly, in a similar spirit. And yet, as the project proceeded, I often found myself pleasantly surprised or unexpectedly moved by an image or a turn of phrase, by the deft execution of a charming lyric or a sustained cry of bitterness from the depths. I found myself increasingly admiring this man who had lived and worked in an enforced but ultimately fruitful isolation, with no apparent concern for literary movements or coteries. I found many pages that are as good as the work of many better-known writers, and many poems that I would be gratified to have written myself, and I am honored to be the medium through which Ennio Contini makes his way to an English-speaking audience.

MICHAEL PALMA

A Brief Journey through the Poetry of Ennio Contini

My sole affliction is to find myself
a stranger in every land. [. . .]
They told me about an island . . .—Lord,
let me not be lost—!
I'll come back to its shore
like a message
bobbed and bandied by the currents.

These lines are by Ennio Contini, who was born in Oristano in 1914 and lived to the age of 92 in Liguria, without ever having returned to his native region. The present volume, a collection that gathers published and unpublished work by Contini, ten years after his death, has come about through the determination of Alfredo de Palchi and the desire to offer a fitting tribute to this forgotten poet who experienced little fame and a great deal of sorrow.

Contini published four volumes of verse in all, from *Magnolia* (1939) through *The Alleluia* (with Ezra Pound, 1952) and *Splinters of Soul* (1962), to *Journey Into the Dark* (1969). In 1995 he published his only novel, *No haya cuartel!*, an exceptional narrative performance in an experimental, Céline-like style.

Contini's family moved to Savona when Ennio was only three years old, and it was here that the young poet took his first steps into the literary environment. From adolescence on, literature and poetry were Contini's sole aspiration, and its beginnings—as he himself ironically recounted—date back to his high school days: "Then, one day, while staying within the rules of meter, I ventured to write a sonnet, called 'Crash'; the crash was that of waves on the sandy beach during stormy days. . . . I was transported for the first time. . . . I read it at school to my classmates and the law professor. And everybody burst out laughing. This, let's say, had been an official debut."[1] Contini's actual debut came when he entered a provincial competition organized by the poets Luigi Pennone and Farfa, and won, with this citation: "Ungarettian. He has a delicate feeling for poetry." For Contini, Ungaretti was the first infatuation and the final inspiration, a poet he carried with him in his prison days and with whom Contini felt he shared the condition of a "man of pain"; in a passage of his diary for September 1947, he wrote from the penitentiary at Procida: "before I fall asleep I'll take up my Ungaretti. . . . [T]here are moments when you need an immediate connection to truth. Only Ungaretti can give me this connection."[2]

Nonetheless, the young poet's literary boundaries needed to range beyond Italy, and Contini, an eager traveler, decided in the years before his army service to go and see other European cities; he visited London, Paris, and Budapest, and it was here, among the crowded cafés of the Hungarian capital, that he made the acquaintance of Ferenc Körmendi, author of *An Adventure in Budapest*. They spent several days discussing literature, art, and Italy, and even now, as evidence of this brief but intense relationship, there remains an epistolary interview[3] in the poet's private archive.

Contini amassed diverse experiences, established relationships with various literary figures, and proceeded to publish his first collection of verse. *Magnolia* appeared in 1939[4] and gathered all the work of his early years; some of its poems are apprentice work, filled with echoes and allusions, but already capable—according to Giorgio Kaisserlian in his preface to the anthology *Postwar Italian Poets*—of stirring "with its own gaze and personal accent."[5] There are hints of his beloved Ungaretti—"End of Summer (Leaves)" is an unspoken but obvious homage; of D'Annunzio (Contini's nature is at times Pan-like, sensual: "The fir trees sink their bodies / into your fluid flesh and alluringly / you gather them in your evening dalliances"); and of Ligurian poets, especially Barile (a line of Contini's, "by a cantabile air at eventide," echoes his best-known work), Sbarbaro, and Montale (between melancholy and slow, sunlit rivers); but Contini is a Ligurian *sui generis*, as pointed out by Giannino Balbis,[6] and in his poetry "one does not find that pain of living that is almost a trademark of the Ligurian school." Contini's landscapes yield a positive message to the reader; memory comes to the rescue like a lifeline; the sea is "clear," gardens are "open," the plunge is "happy"; even these earliest of his poems contain an element that will characterize Contini as man and poet—namely, hope, which is vested in the last lines of the collection: "In your / Mediterranean zone, I bloom."

An abyss separates the poems of *Magnolia* from those of *The Alleluia*, published in 1952.[7] An abyss made of pain and suffering, but also of reading and profound changes. Ennio Contini enlisted in the army and was at first sent to officer training school at Salerno, before moving on to the 41st infantry regiment stationed at Imperia. Here Lieutenant Contini was assigned as an instructor in a refresher course on new automatic weapons, and among his pupils he came to know the poet Renzo Laurano (born Luigi Asquasciati): "Laurano was a slightly inattentive student, but I leaned on him. Then he recited one of his most beautiful poems." The friendship between the two—born "in uniform" in 1937 and lasting until the death of the author of *Chiara Laughs* in 1986—allowed the young Contini to come in contact with some of the most important literary personalities of the period (Salvatore Quasimodo, Bonaventura Tecchi, and Adriano Grande, to name only a few) and to publish stories and poems in various nationally known journals, including *Meridiano di Roma*, *Circoli*, and *Cynthia*. Then along came the front, distancing Contini from his literary ambitions: that of Albania, where the young lieutenant was sent into combat on the plain of Tepeleni; and it was here, through a random quirk of fate, that he encountered his older brother Umberto.[8] A soldier among soldiers knows the horror of war and the most deeply buried fears of the human spirit; literature is only a distant echo: "[A] shell exploded right in the middle of our encampment . . . from every part of the camp rose invocations and the heartrending cry of 'Mamma'! . . . The rain of fire and blood lasted until nearly six in the evening"; and again: "And my name was called out, as if the Major, instead of telling me that I had to move my platoon up to the front line, wanted to tell me: 'I'll give you literature!'" Back from the front after being wounded in battle, Contini underwent a long period of convalescence between Savona and Genoa, and it was then that he dedicated himself to literature with a renewed passion: in these years he read Eliot, Joyce, and Pound, and also Gide, Mauriac, and Godoy, and reread the classics and the Bible: "[P]oetry is my soul, literature is my bread." Along with articles principally devoted to literary criticism (*Meridiano di Roma* issued his essays on Laurano, Schaub, and Godoy[9]) Contini—using the pseudonym Enrico Cortini—published lighter pieces in journals such as *Novella* and *Grazia*. Once again, however, it was the war that diverted the poet from his calling and—to paraphrase Contini himself—dragged him far from his "soul" and his "bread." Because of incidents related to his function as an army lieutenant and having been arrested as a war criminal ("in the dreams of a poet there is also room for the Fatherland, and this, which for me turned out to be the most deceptive dream, this dream, I say, influenced much of my life"), Contini was tried and condemned to death. His sentence, later commuted to life, was finally modified to nine years' incarceration in the prisons of Savona, Procida, and Civitavecchia. Crushed by "political passions and by an anxious and adventurous life," as he wrote to his friend Bonaventura Tecchi, Contini in 1945 came to know what Renzo Laurano has described as "civil death": prison scarred him deeply, as a man and a poet; it was an experience that branded his life indelibly. But Contini did not lose heart, and even in prison literature was his lifeline. During the years of his detention at Civitavecchia (1951–1953), the interesting correspondence that links Contini to Ezra Pound was resumed; the two men had met in Rapallo in 1939[10] and they had both contributed to *Meridiano di Roma* between 1938 and 1943.

By a strange twist of fate, Contini, imprisoned at Civitavecchia, wrote to the master poet Ezra Pound, himself confined at St. Elizabeths mental hospital in Washington, D.C., and from this brief exchange of letters came the idea of publishing Contini's *The Alleluia* together with the first decade of Pound's *Cantos*. The first letter, from Contini to Pound, dates from Christmas 1950, and contains one of the most beautiful lyrics that would appear in the collection, "Lord, the Wall Has Risen," dedicated to Pound: "Dearest poet, now with our sixth Christmas in prison approaching, on behalf of the honest faction of Italian poets, I offer you my best wishes. . . . Out of my admiration for you, I include a poem of mine dedicated to you—Courage!" In 1951 Contini wrote: "Dear master and friend. . . . We also talked about all that I mean to do for a comeback of your poetry in Italy (translations and presentations in various journals and a volume of your and my poems[11]—this at the earliest)"; in 1952 the volume was ready: "so our book, *The Alleluia*, will see the light between the 20th and the 25th of April of this year, in other words, in about twenty days. It will have a notable success in the press: our most important critics will be interested in our book. I can tell you that as of today more than 200 copies of *The Alleluia* have already been ordered. . . . The book, as I have written you, will have a very elegant appearance and will be displayed in the principal Italian bookstores: it will be reviewed by our most illustrious literary critics: Bonaventura Tecchi and Emilio Cecchi, as well as a myriad of minor reviewers."

Casimiro Fabbri, the publisher of the collection, wrote to Contini: "P. P. Pasolini has even told me that he has admired your poetry, I don't know if and where he will say so. This will give you a lift, because as you know he is very critical."[12] The publication had had a moderate success and *The Alleluia* was commented on in print by Renzo Laurano, Bonaventura Tecchi, Luigi Pennone, and Francesco Piselli, among others; but Contini wrote a few years later, after Pound's (and his own) incarceration had ended: "No one remembered about me that I had, against my every interest but with much affection, extricated the great American poet from the limbo into which he had been plunged with his internment in the hospital for the criminally insane in Washington." Contini, however, was the only person who could boast of a joint publication with Pound, and *The Alleluia* will remain a *unicum* in the literary history of its author.

In the Contini poems contained in this volume, all the innovations and suggestions born of new European tendencies flow together in an original way;

we find references to Gide, Valéry, and Eliot, but they are well amalgamated in the poet's own very strong voice. Contini's lyrics are life as it is lived and life as it should be, "from the harshest realism to the most unashamed sincerity," and they ask a remarkable level of empathy from the reader. Prison confines the poet within the the bounds of a cell ("for five years . . . I have gray eyes / from too much staring at rocks"), but not his spirit ("Today we are dead / to live tomorrow"); still, there is torment, and the poet feels himself to be "crucified / by my brothers for a handful of mud" when the river presents a "regurgitation of slimy / and bitter algae / . . . to my thirst." Contini is young ("I carry thirty-five / springtimes in my heart") and already knows the "chill of death," but he is able to rise and look ahead, past the gray wall that blocks his gaze, aware "of having paid for the gift of life, / like a Lord, with blood." Even in this circumstance, the collection *The Alleluia* concludes with a hopeful ode; Contini knows that he can be born into a new life: "Oh people, / wash the body / ready for the loves of the Lord, / and provide unguents and spikenard / and alleluia / ALLELUIA!"

With *Splinters of Soul* (1962)[13]—combining poems selected from *Magnolia* and *The Alleluia* with unpublished ones—Contini was reborn as a man and as a poet, inaugurating that phase of rereading himself that would characterize the final stages of his poetry. In the preface to the volume, Adriano Grande coined for Contini the epithet "clearest of hermetics," for the quality in his lyrics of tending toward a hermetic purity while at the same time expressing nothing "that is not based on an experience lived in the heart as well as the imagination." In an interview dating back to the 1980s, in reference to his relationship with the Hermetics, Contini states: "[W]hen speaking of the hermeticism of Ennio Contini I tend always to specify one point. It isn't that I lived through the Italian hermetic season of Quasimodo and Gatto. . . . I have always renewed myself with French Symbolism. . . . Baudelaire, Rimbaud, Mallarmé." For Grande, *Splinters of Soul* is a collection that directly places Ennio Contini among the leading poets of the twentieth century "for its illumination of his originality, which is of a strongly pronounced nature, in contrast to the legions of hermetic versifiers, both past and present." In the lyrics of this collection we retrace the stages that the poet has passed through to this point; prison is a grievous wound embedded in his memory that continues to somehow brand his present life: "Recollection is a dam / that aches"; still, Contini can go beyond and draw inspiration from the new reality that surrounds him. It is not by chance that the dedication that opens the collection is "To Maria," the lifelong companion whom Contini had met shortly after his imprisonment; in marriage, family, and the birth of their two daughters, Contini found new peace and renewed impulse: "You are my father and my mother / the brother / who lends a hand / a home / to memory / . . . / From the vagrant that I am / . . . / only in you I recover myself." The moments of despondency recur and are frequently compared to rain that falls suddenly and incessantly, even in summer; and in "House in Liguria," dedicated to Contini's mother, regrets tap at the poet's door "like stripped-away / leaves."

In the section called "Further Adventures," made up of poems written between 1946 and 1959, we find a piece explicitly titled "To My Wife" that splendidly encompasses the whole human and poetic journey that Contini has lived to this point. Maria has become for him a symbol of purity and rebirth: "The sickness that was in me / . . . / I have burned off / in the pure amphora / of your youth."

In 1969, with the publication of *Journey Into the Dark*,[14] Contini closes the circle, and he chooses to do so, once again, with a collection. Cesare Garelli, author of the preface, rightly indicates how "Contini has a recurrent need to take stock of himself, in a repeated search for his own human and poetic authenticity." The title recalls the much more famous *Journey to the End of Night* by Louis-Ferdinand Céline, which Contini had avidly read. Here the journey into the dark is that of the poet into his past, his memory, and his great sorrow, in an attempt to make peace with himself as a sailor who has spent "the last penny of [his] pay / at the tavern of memories." Contini starts once again from his prison and his adopted land ("The wind was swelling the laundry hanging up / in the dormitory room. Memory ran / backward toward the agaves / and lemons of Liguria") and opens the collection with a nostalgic and Montalean lyric (the echoes of "lemon trees" and "the agave that roots itself in the crevice" are obvious); subsequently come poems reprinted—without titles—from *The Alleluia* and *Splinters of Soul*, almost as if to test the reader's memory. The lyrics follow one another in no precise order, the dates follow no chronological sequence, and for scanning the rhythm of the collection there is only the tempo of the spirit. Garelli underlines how important it is to dwell on the value "of the existential itinerary" that this volume posseses: Contini accompanies us on this journey, which is his journey, but could also be ours. At the end of the collection, the poet gives us a previously unpublished poem, "Evening Mass," inspired by the Pär Lagerkvist novel *Barabbas*; in it, to quote Garelli, "one ends up prefering the sinister grandeur of the seller of Christ to the dull conformism of today's believers"; but it is the same Contini who reveals to us the true essence of poetry: "the matrix was this and nothing but this: the indifference and indolence of man in the face of the spirit." Indolence that Contini always pushed back against through a great strength of spirit (he writes in an unpublished diary: "I have a patience that is deep and tenacious as the earth") that led him always to redeem himself from every situation and to rise again even when life seemed to have nothing in store for him but suffering. It is not by chance that *Journey Into the Dark* concludes with this poem in which sin and resurrection find an admirable balance, that of the poet who has been able to accept by way of reconciliation his own tormented existence, "reconciliation as a manly sentiment of awareness, an acknowledged recapitulation of good and evil and pains suffered and inflicted (and thus in any case lived)."

In *No haya cuartel!*,[15] his only published work of prose, Contini traces the stages of the childhood and youth of his protagonist Quirino Biddau amid innocence, profanity, and obsessions. Family vicissitudes are narrated with extreme irony, grotesque and visionary shadings, and recourse to a Céline-like experimental style,[16] a style, as Umberto Rapallo says in the afterword to the volume, rich with "cultural echoes and intertexts, which alternate with moments of high lyricism."

In the years between the publication of *Journey Into the Dark* in 1969 and the publication of his only novel in 1995, Contini did not abandon poetry, as shown by the numerous unpublished texts collected in this volume, poems that testify to the great vitality of a writer reborn into a new life, of a poet filled with the hope that "at dawn / emerald will blossom on the meadow."

FRANCESCA BERGADANO

1. Unpublished notebooks of Ennio Contini, from the Contini family private archive.
2. Unpublished prison diary, from the Contini family private archive.
3. "Dear Sir, I hereby reply at once to your kind letter; first of all to your questions. . . . [O]ne of the greatest satisfactions of my work as a writer is how my books have been received by the Italian public. . . . You ask if I like Italy? Yes, sir! Not only as a landscape but also with some regard to the other aspects of life. . . . Thank you once again for your kind interest, your most devoted Ferenc Körmendi" (autograph letter dated October 15, 1935; from the Contini family private archive).
4. Ennio Contini, *Magnolia*, Emiliano degli Orfini 1939.
5. Giorgio Kaisserlian, ed., *Poeti italiani del secondo dopoguerra*, Guido Miano 1958, p. 61.
6. Giannino Balbis, "Ennio Contini e il poema della speranza," in *Val Bormida. Storia e cultura*, n. 4, 1988, 127–129.
7. Ennio Contini, *L'Alleluja, con la prima decade dei Cantos di Ezra Pound*, Società Editrice Siciliana 1952.

8. "I'm hungry—he told me—so I made him a hot soup: that is to say, I took the mess tin, put in water, an onion, and a small can of meat, lit a candle under the tin and heated up the poultice. Running into your brother at the front is something that can't be described with rhetoric" (unpublished diaries of Ennio Contini, from the Contini family private archive).
9. Contini's essays in *Meridiano di Roma* on Renzo Laurano, Emil Schaub, and Armand Godoy appeared as follows: Laurano, August 7, 1938, p. IV; Godoy, September 25, 1938, p. IX; Schaub, March 26, 1939, p. IX.
10. For the meeting between them in Rapallo we have Contini's own account, in a 1986 video, stored in the Contini archive and transferred to digital format: "I met Ezra Pound in 1939 in Rapallo, where he lived. Even before that we knew each other by sight, so to speak, because we both published in *Meridiano di Roma*, which had by then taken the place of *Fiera Letteraria*. He contributed articles on economics, on the American economy, and I contributed brief essays on foreign literature."
11. One of the most beautiful Contini lyrics in the collection is *Signore, il muro è cresciuto* ("Lord, the Wall Has Risen"), itself dedicated to Ezra Pound.
12. Pasolini is not known to have written anything about Contini.
13. Ennio Contini, *Schegge d'anima*, preface by Adriano Grande, Carpena 1962.
14. Ennio Contini, *Viaggio nel buio*, preface by Cesare Garelli, Sabatelli 1969.
15. Ennio Contini, *No haya cuartel!*, afterword by Umberto Rapallo, Edizioni dell'Orso, 1995.
16. Typically Céline-like is the obsessive use of ellipses, which Contini masterfully reworks: "Mammà turns on him puffing like a viper, she bites him on the hand . . . He opens his eyes to the future . . . He sobs . . . This can't go on . . . He collapses. . . ."

da MAGNOLIA (1939)

from MAGNOLIA (1939)

A luna piena

A luna piena, parlò più forte
al silenzio l'argentea voce dei rivi.

Poi, sospirava suo fresco languore,
sui docili fili dell'erba,
muta la rugiada.

All'alba
fiorirà sul prato lo smeraldo.

At the Full Moon

At the full moon, the silvery voice
of brooks spoke louder to the silence.

Then the hushed dew sighed its cool
languor on the docile
blades of grass.

                    At dawn
emerald will blossom on the meadow.

Isolotto di Bergeggi

(su un ritmo della felicità, di Kennedy)

L'isola mia è tranquilla
tra musiche onde, sui letti
abissali ove il verde oltremare
tremola al sole e scintilla.

« Giuochi anche tu? Vieni
nell'onda! »
                    e mi tuffo, felice,
nei gorghi d'opale
dietro la scia luminosa.

Mi poso, poi,
alla mia algosa riviera.
Tentatrice una conchiglia sonora
mi màcera il tempo.

L'isola mia è bella,
stasera; le sirene in sordina
la cullano. Mosso andantino.

Islet of Bergeggi

(on a joyful rhythm, by Kennedy)

My island is tranquil
amid musical waves, over unfathomable
beds where green from beyond the sea
shimmers in the sun and sparkles.

"Are you playing too? Come on
into the wave!"
                    and I plunge, happy,
into the opal eddies
behind the luminous wake.

I settle, then,
along my algal shore.
A temptress shell sounds,
time macerates me.

My island is lovely,
this evening; sirens are silently
rocking it. Andantino mosso.

Nebbia

Umida e sinuosa amante.

Gli abeti affondano i loro corpi
nelle tue fluide carni e procace
l'accogli nei tuoi amori serali.

Ma come frale è tua carne
e nei tuoi grigi desiri volubile,
ti distendi nel naufragar della notte
a nuovi vergini lidi,
nebbia —
                                e, il guardiano dell'aurora
ti spinge come i mercanti dal tempio
di tra le colonne della navata canora
lontana dal sole
dalla innocente chiarità dei mattini.

Fog

Moist and sinuous mistress.

The fir trees sink their bodies
into your fluid flesh and alluringly
you gather them in your evening dalliances.

But how frail is your flesh
and in your inconstant gray desires,
you spread out in the foundering of the night
toward new virgin shores,
fog—
        and, the watchman of the dawn
drives you like the moneychangers from the temple
from between the columns of the resonant nave
far from the sun
from the innocent clarity of mornings.

Fine d'estate (foglie)

Sonno nell'aria
e intristiscono i faggi: gocce di sangue
— perdute reminiscenze
d'un amplesso che stagna ormai
alla foce tranquilla.

Un brivido, ancora, li arpeggia,
lento, quasi un piccolo sasso
c'affonda in trasparenze marine
e si posa
tra alghe stanche e rossi
arborati coralli.

Coriandoli dai tremori
canori
legàti ancora alle fronde
da un lieve sorriso di vita.

Non siete ancora fantàsime,
timide ombre fluite
sulla terra riarsa: cenere
— e carnevale è finito.

End of Summer (Leaves)

Sleep in the air
and the beeches are wilting: drops of blood
—lost reminiscences
of an embrace that's stagnating by now
at the tranquil estuary.

A shiver still plays them like a harp,
slow, as though a little stone
sinks in marine transparencies
and settles
amid weary algae and red
arbored corals.

Confetti from resonant
tremors
still tied to the branches
by a faint smile of life.

You are still not phantoms,
timid shadows fluttered
over the parched earth: ashes
—and the carnival is finished.

A Fulvia

Neppure tu fanciulla
mi porterai nel sole

soffoca il pianto
l'anima

di lontano vedo
barriere

nebbie pesanti
se grido
nulla mi ode

vita
io
ti dispero

resto nell'ansia folle
turgide
vene

neppure tu fanciulla
mi porterai nel sole

To Fulvia

Not even you my girl
will carry me into the sun

tears smother
the spirit

from far off I see
barriers

thick fogs
if I cry out
nothing hears me

life
I
despair of you

I'm mired in mad anxiety
swollen
veins

not even you my girl
will carry me into the sun

Domenicale

Adagiata su di un muro sottile
— la chioma di fanciulla stupefatta
cullata
da un'aria cantabile di primasera —
una magnolia s'attarda in sogno
sulla via, da un giardino.

Sunday

Set carefully on a slender wall
—the hair of a dazzled little girl
lulled
by a cantabile air at eventide—
a magnolia tarries in a dream
along the way, from a garden.

Verginità di Ina

Ina ricama nel sole
i suoi tredicianni — Io
sono bambina — ti dice; s'accarezza
i castani capelli e in un sorriso ti parla:
— sono fatta così.
                    Nessuno
mi turba le oasi azzurre
ed in ogni sentiero
intreccio passi di danza in merletti
e trine d'Olanda.

La mia riviera è lenta,
assolata, canta alla sua breve proda
una lieve risacca e solo Ina
può andare in barchetta
in questo primaverile mare
di freschezza.

S'incanta Ina ad un gioco
— può essere l'amore? — s'indugia,
sorride, v'intreccia le dita di luna
sulla bocca — perché non sa —
e sparisce.

Ina è fatta così — Vi guarda, s'incanta,
vi canta l'amore e non più.
Ina è come la luna
sorride
e rimane lassù.

Ina's Maidenhood

In the sun Ina embroiders
her thirteen years: —I
am a child, she says to you; she strokes
her chestnut hair and tells you with a smile:
—that's what I am.
                    No one
disturbs my blue oases
and on every pathway
I interweave dance steps in tatting
and Dutch lace braids.

My coast is calm,
sunny, it sings a soft undertow
to the nearby shore and only Ina
can set out in a little boat
in this springtime sea
of freshness.

Ina enchants herself into a game
—can it be love?—she lingers,
smiles, interweaves your moon fingers
over her mouth—she doesn't know why—
and disappears.

That's what Ina is—She looks at you all, enchanted,
sings to you of love and nothing more.
Ina is like the moon
she smiles
and stays up above.

Tu sei racchiusa

Tu sei racchiusa quasi
in sonora conchiglia,
le onde della vita sciabordano
alla tua riva bianca.

Se affiso il tuo volto
un'agonia di carezze
preme le mie docili tempia.

Nella radura azzurra
ombrata dalle tue palmate ciglia
tremula un sorriso
e smèmora.
                    Alla tua plaga
mediterranea, fiorisco.

You Are Enclosed

You are enclosed, nearly,
in a sonorous shell,
the waves of life are lapping
at your white shore.

If I fixate on your face
an agony of caresses
presses my docile temples.

In the blue glade
shaded by your palmate lashes
a smile glimmers and
goes blank.
                    In your
Mediterranean zone, I bloom.

POESIE INEDITE
(1939–1942)

UNCOLLECTED POEMS
(1939–1942)

È notturna foresta il tuo divenire

a Armand Godoy

È notturna foresta il tuo divenire.
Ebbro delle tue stesse passioni tu cerchi
vanamente l'orlo dell'abisso, l'estasi
tacita ove s'appaci il tuo delirare.
Ed il tremore dei bianchi ruscelli, le voci
le mille voci sonore — o vita o vita —
ti peseranno, gelide, quasi
fiera predata dall'onda dei tuoi stessi rimorsi.
Invano riposerai, vagabondo dei tuoi ruvidi sangui.
Invano cercherai nell'oblio delle cose passate
un sollievo alla presente amarezza, invano
— effimera argilla — ti cullerai alla brezza
stupefacente delle rosee, delle dolci illusioni.

E scenderà la sera. La tua squallida sera.

1939

A Forest in the Dark Is Your Becoming

to Armand Godoy

A forest in the dark is your becoming.
Drunk on your own passions you go searching
in vain for the edge of the abyss, the silent
ecstasy where your raving's pacified.
And the shivering of white streams, the voices
the thousand resonant voices—O life O life—
will weigh icily on you, almost
a wild beast attacked by the surge of your own regrets.
You will rest in vain, vagabond of your rugged bloodlines.
You will search in vain in forgetfulness of things past
for a balm to your present bitterness, you will sway
in vain—ephemeral clay—to the narcotic
breeze of roseate and sweet illusions.

And evening will descend. Your desolate evening.

1939

Bengala alle mie nozze

Notte aperta e d'innumerevoli stelle.

Sulla quieta marina
a tenue bava di aria s'appendeva una
sonnolenta estate.

Lucciolavano lampare, al largo.

E su di un letto di rena si tace
docile sangue d'una ragazza.

                    Dalle magnolie
fioriscono i bengala alle mie nozze.

Bengal Lights at My Wedding

Clear night of innumerable stars.

On the serene seacoast
a somnolent summer hung by a
faint puff of air.

Fishing lamps were fireflying, from afar.

And upon a bed of sand the docile
blood of a girl is keeping still.

                    Among the magnolias
Bengal lights are blossoming at my wedding.

Mi zampillano in cuore i quattro salti
matti ch'io facevo da fanciullo sulla tiepida rena
della mia riviera.
Rosso come un gambero dal sole estivo, tra i flutti
freschi della marina. E là, che marinaro io ero
intrepido alle onde bruciato dal sole e dal sale
nell'aria limpida della mia città di Liguria.
O marinaro, come sei vecchio ora e quanta
nostalgia nel tuo cuore naufragato. E tua madre?
Mia madre lontana senza più lacrime
mia morte lenta, ti ricordo sempre mia carne
e sento la tua voce velata: — figlio mio!
Bisogna ch'io rida come un pagliaccio da circo
per dimenticare. Per non morire impallidito
dalla crescente tristezza di questa mia terribile vita
d'esiliato.
Altro mare mi circonda, ora, un alto mare
ch'io difficile assaggio, straniero ad altri amici
ed alla sera mi sento senza una casa.
Oh non mi si spenga il tenue viso di mia madre
ancora morire nel suo ricordo, ancora, mio Dio.
Quando, a salti di tempo, mi zampillano in cuore
i quattro salti fatti da fanciullo sulla tiepida rena
della mia riviera, io solo allora faccio festa
di calde lacrime e rivedo mia madre.

Zara, 5 maggio 1942

Welling up in my heart are the four wild leaps
I made when I was a boy on the lukewarm sand
of my shore.
Red as a lobster from the summer sun, amid the cool
coastal waves. And there, what a sailor I was
bold in the billows burned by the sun and the salt
In the pure air of my Ligurian city.
O sailor, how old you've grown now and how much
nostalgia in your shipwrecked heart. And your mother?
My mother so far away with no tears left
my slow death, I think of you always my flesh and blood
and always hear your veiled voice saying "My son!"
I should be laughing like a circus clown
so as to forget. So as not to die bled white
by the deepening sorrow of my wretched life
of exile.
Another sea surrounds me now, a high sea
hard for me to taste, foreign to other friends,
and in the evening I feel like a homeless man.
Oh may my mother's faint face not fade from me
to die once more in memory, once more, my God.
When, in the leaps of time, they well up in my heart,
the four wild leaps of a boy on the lukewarm sand
of my shore, only then do I make a feast
of warm tears and see my mother's face again.

Zara, May 5, 1942

POESIE INEDITE
(1946–1953)

(scritte durante la prigionia nelle carceri di Savona, Procida, e Civitavecchia)

UNCOLLECTED POEMS
(1946–1953)

(written during imprisonment in the jails of Savona, Procida, and Civitavecchia)

Mi rimane
in questo pallido inferno
ultimo dono gelida
parola.

Gli effimeri giorni e l'ora
rosario d'angeli fiochi
io deliro
in questo stormire di conchiglia

Ai suoi limiti fermi
mio sangue trascolora fiaba
ch'era dolce mito
di verdi stagioni

Signore, ho la tua pena
in questa cella sacrilega.

30 gennaio 1946

I have left
in this pallid inferno
one last gift an icy
word.

The ephemeral days and the hour
a rosary of dim angels
I am raving
in this rustling of a shell

At its fixed limits
my blood discolors a fable
that was a sweet myth
of green seasons

Lord, I share your suffering
in this sacrilegious cell.

January 30, 1946

A insidiarmi il sangue ritorni
e di dolcezze sogno
esiliato tra queste quattro mura —

Era tuo frutto tra verdeggianti siepi
goloso ai tiepidi tramonti
di seni facevo trepida avventura
tradito da veniente sera

Nascita di primavera nella luna
svaniva su una bava di seta
in canto quieto di grilli

Ancora una luce tremola
in musica di sangui ora
che ti so rapita, e in me si spegne eco
di tuo pianto querulo,
isola verde, amore.

30 gennaio 1946

You return to ensnare my blood
and I dream of sweetness
exiled inside these four walls—

Your fruit was amid the verdant hedges
avid at tepid sunsets
I made an anxious adventure of breasts
betrayed by approaching evening

Springtime's moonlight birth
vanished on a floss of silk
in the quiet song of crickets

A light still flickers
in the music of bloods now that
I know you are swept away, and in me dies the echo
of your mournful lamentation,
green island, love.

January 30, 1946

Signore, esiliami dall'ansia
di questo corpo terroso
dammi pensiero nudo e dolce
di vento tra scarni ulivi.

Signore,
toglimi l'angosciata musica
delle vene e tepide sere in cui
altalena di luna
dava vertigine di donne —
ch'io emigri da questa crocifissa carne
in volo spento di cigni
d'orfico mito

Signore, misericordia.

In questa esperienza umana
in questa armonia di sangui e d'universo
Signore ho udito la tua parola
che fece della mia esperienza umana
un'armonia di sangui e d'universo —

E nella ricerca del bene ebbi
dal male la luce del tuo bene
o prima o troppo tardi
nel giusto punto ho sofferto —

Ma sempre la tua musica,
ora fioca ora in altissimo crescendo,
mi districò dai rami e vissi
da uomo vicino alla sorgente —

Lord, exile me from the anxiety
of this earthy body
bestow on me the sweet and naked thought
of wind between the scrawny olive trees.

Lord,
take from me the anguished music of
the veins and tepid evenings when
a moonlight swing
made me grow dizzy over women—
that I may emigrate from this crucified flesh
in a lifeless flight of swans
of Orphic myth

Lord, have mercy.

In this human experience
in this harmony of bloods and universe
Lord I have heard your word
that made my human experience
a harmony of bloods and universe—

And in the search for goodness I have had
out of evil the light of your goodness
either before or too late
I have suffered as I should—

But always your music,
now faint now in the highest of crescendos,
disentangled me from the branches
and I lived near the wellspring of man—

E quando il cuore era sereno
t'amai, Signore, e ti perdetti,
solo per poco forse una volta,
quando il mio cuore era morso dalla noia —

Vissi come era giusto vivere
da uomo fatto a somiglianza
di Cristo ch'era Tuo figlio;
del Tuo sangue e del Tuo pane mi cibai —

Altri uomini dissero
ch'era strano dagli altri il mio vivere
ma non ne feci caso;
una bandiera avevo da seguire.

E come mutano i giorni e gli alberi
così cangiarono i pensieri umani
di un'antica favola che
già nel mio sangue trascolora —

E asceso il Calvario di Tuo Figlio
io sono crocifisso dai dolci fratelli
per un pugno di fango.
Non mi ribello, Signore, ho la tua sorte —

T'invoco per i dolci fratelli umani,
Signore, misericordia.

Savona il 6 febbraio 1946

And when my heart was at peace
I loved you, Lord, and I lost you
once, perhaps, just for a short while,
when my heart was eaten up by boredom—

I lived as it was right for man to live,
man who has been fashioned in the image
of Christ who was Your son;
on Your blood and on Your bread I fed myself—

Other men said
my way of life was odd to others
but I put no stock in it;
I had a flag to follow.

And as the days turned and the trees with them
so did they change, the human thoughts
about an ancient fable that
is already changing color in my blood—

And I have climbed the Calvary of Your Son
I am crucified by my sweet brothers
for a handful of mud.
I do not protest, Lord, I share your lot—

I call to you for my sweet human brothers,
Lord, have mercy.

Savona, February 6, 1946

Interno

E so quello che non posso ridire,
oltre il balbettare delle sillabe,
macerarmi in questo pugno di carne,
antico e silenzioso come un dio.

E tremola in questa fossa profonda,
come un occhio di mare opalescente,
la mia voce sopita di colomba.

Quale trenino di campagna in larghi
ciuffi di reseda serpeggia pigro,
nel crepuscolo del paese incantato,
la pallida fiaba del mio sangue.

12 aprile 1946

Interior

And I know something I cannot repeat,
beyond the stuttering of syllables,
macerating me within this fist
of flesh, ancient and silent as a god.

And it is quivering in this deep ditch,
like an eye in an opalescent sea,
this voice of mine that is muted as a dove's.

Like a small train winding lazily across
the countryside in the abundant clumps
of reseda, in the twilight of the enchanted
land, the pallid fable of my blood.

April 12, 1946

Madonna, tu che sei dolce Madre
al Figliolo ch'ai pianto
sotto la Croce crudele — Madonna
che sette piaghe porti nel cuore
nostro dolore
a questo pianto china
il tuo viso di giglio, alla sofferta
mia sera tendi la pietosa mano.

Ho creduto essere un dio
alla mia vita svagata
ed ora non sono che un tremore segreto
nella mia argilla domata.

Madre pietosa,
Perdona questo mio mito folle
questo mio sangue che bolle
ancora di segreti peccati, perdona.

Madre, umilissima Madre
del Figliolo divino
ascolta questo mio pianto — Madre
in ginocchio ti prego
in ginocchio ti chiedo,
Madre, la pace.

Savona 1946

Madonna, you who are the tender Mother
of the Son for whom you wept
under the cruel Cross—Madonna
who carry seven wounds within your heart
our pain
bend your lily face
to this weeping, extend
your merciful hand to my tormented evening.

I believed myself to be a god
of my daydreaming life
and now I'm nothing but a secret tremor
in my subdued sod.

Merciful Mother,
forgive this mad myth of mine
and forgive this blood of mine
that still boils with secret sins.

Mother, most humble Mother
of the divine beloved Son
hear this weeping of mine—Mother
on my knees I pray to you
on my knees I beg of you,
Mother, grant me peace.

Savona, 1946

Moscone ronza e batte

E al risveglio mi torna solita alba
e tardi pomeriggi di mosche
pigre e amaro di ricordi.

Solo, noiosa estate trascino
in ruvidità di sangui conchiusi
da un'ora morta, immote palme.

E tornano voci sfocate: moscone
ronza e batte indefinitamente
su mia vetrosa anima: chiudo
fiaba terrena in questo mondo di sabbia
abbacinante.

Nel deserto della mia carne
m'appacio sugli ultimi fili di erba
arsi.

Procida 1947

A Bluebottle Buzzes and Beats

And when I wake the usual dawn returns
to me and late afternoons of lazy
flies and bitter with memories.

Alone, I drag myself through tedious summer
in the roughness of bloodlines brought to an end
by a dead hour, motionless palm trees.

And indistinct voices return: a bluebottle
buzzes and beats indefinitely
on my vitreous spirit: I enclose
an earthly fable in this world of dazzling
sand.

In the desert of my flesh
I appease myself on the last burnt blades
of grass.

Procida, 1947

Perché ora è la sera

Giobbe, seduto sulla roccia, piange:
Dove sono i regni,
le primavere dell'infanzia,
le cattedrali della giovinezza . . .
Dove sono caduto?

Passeggiando per sentieri tortuosi
impediti dalle ragnatele del Settembre.
Pioverà oggi?
Dovrei mettermi un farsetto più pesante
e inginocchiarmi sotto l'albero della vita.
Ti prego, Signore, conducimi per mano.

La sera incombe.
La cenere sale dal rogo della mia anima,
squittisce come un topo,
si frange con rumor di vetri sul selciato.
Con lampade di fuoco i bar risucchiano
gli ultimi avventori.

La sera si insinua con lingue tenere di donna.
Ho perduto tutto . . .
Con lingue di fuoco, e tenere, la sera . . .
Settembre cade
con un tonfo di rimorsi e di ricordi.

Giobbe piange, il volto nella polvere.
Salendo le scale di casa,
tra orina di gatti e foglie di basilico.

Because Now It Is Evening

Job, as he sits upon the rock, cries out:
Where are the kingdoms,
the springtimes of childhood,
the cathedrals of youth . . .
Where have I fallen?

Making my way along the twisting paths
hindered by the cobwebs of September.
Will it rain today?
I ought to put a heavier jacket on
and kneel down underneath the tree of life.
I beg you, Lord, please lead me by the hand.

Evening looms.
Ashes rise from the pyre of my soul,
squeal like a mouse,
break with the sound of glass on the cobblestones.
With lamps of flame the coffeeshops suck in
their final customers.

Evening insinuates itself with the tender tongues of women.
I have lost everything . . .
With tongues of flame, and tenderly, the evening . . .
September falls
with the thudding of regrets and recollections.

Job cries out and weeps, his face in the dust.
Climbing the stairs of the house,
amid the cat piss and the basil leaves.

Non ho tempo da perdere.
Spingo l'uscio ed entro . . .

Perché Tu sei la nostra salvezza.

Più che l'azione è la meditazione.
Più che la meditazione è la Parola.
Usala.
La folla non ti capisce.
Siedi e attendi.

Tra mormorio di acque, dal lavello
giunge il lamento di Giobbe.
È nel deserto,
tra occhi che spiano il tormento.
La mia parola, Signore, è vento
gonfio tra mondi che oscillano
e si frangono ai Tuoi piedi.

Perché ora è la sera
e il tuo lamento coagula tra i vicoli,
ombra sull'ombra,
di uno squallido autunno.

Perché ora sei tu e tu solo
e le tue lacrime, Giobbe, non giovano ad alcuno.
Sei vento tra le imposte sconnesse,
fumo sui candelieri appena spenti.

La Messa è finita.
Andate in pace.

1950

I have no time to lose.
I push the door open and go in . . .

Because You are our salvation.

More than the action is the meditation.
More than the meditation is the Word.
Use it.
The crowd doesn't understand you.
Sit and wait.

Amid the murmur of waters, from the sink
comes the lament of Job.
He is in the desert,
watched by eyes that spy on his torment.
My word, Lord, is a wind
swollen between worlds that oscillate
and break up at Your feet.

Because now it is evening
and your lament is curdling in the alleys,
shadow on shadow,
of a squalid autumn.

Because now you are you and only you
and your tears, Job, are no use to anyone.
You are wind between disjointed shutters,
smoke on candlesticks already snuffed.

The Mass is ended.
Go in peace.

1950

Due poesie per P. (1950)

I

Le sue sembianze che il vento ha informemente accolto
estate, la dolce, a te l'affida
finché il tuo labbro al ramo verde e all'acqua pura beva
il margine fiorito d'ogni prato.
A tanto celeste segno, l'occhio volto al cielo
e a queste bizzose acacie protese all'orizzonte,
fantasia ti ritrova, o mia dai grandi occhi lucenti.
Mi riconforta, e avrà di certo un senso
che il tempo non ha roso
l'indifferenza fresca dei gelsi, ora che nei tuoi occhi
la pianura prosegue più che in se stessa.
Insieme dunque ci si addentra nell'idea preziosa della vita
e in chiarezza ci accoglie il sole ovunque acceso.

II

Il veliero che liberi nel cuore
al dolce vento muta il giro;
volge all'oro staccato dai declivi
l'ombra del sole e al labbro della sera
l'onda slarga il mare.
All'incantato fischio dell'ultimo battello
la rondine si bagna, discende
al cieco limite della riva
alla terrazza sulla casa.

Two Poems for P. (1950)

I

Summer, the sweet, entrusts to you its features which
the wind has shapelessly welcomed
until your lip at the green branch and the pure water
drinks the flowery edge of every meadow.
At so heavenly a sign, the eye turned to the sky
and to these frisky acacias stretched toward the horizon,
a fancy finds you anew, O my one with the great gleaming eyes.
It refreshes me, and surely it will make sense
that time has not gnawed away
the cool indifference of the mulberries, now that the plain
persists more in your eyes than in itself.
And so together we penetrate into the precious idea of life
and in clarity the sun welcomes us wherever it is lit.

II

The sailing ship you set free in the heart
shifts course in the gentle wind;
the shadow of the sun turns to gold
pulled from the slopes and at the edge of evening
the wave enlarges the sea.
At the enchanted whistle of the last boat
the swallow bathes, and descends
to the lightless boundary of the shore
by the terrace of the house.

Non so più quale memoria ti canti
ora che nelle mani mi è rimasta
la pioggia fredda di salmastro
e porto il segno delle correnti chiare negli occhi.
È la tristezza che ci sperde il volto,
mia immagine d'aria, e a chi ti cerca
rimane in sogno l'antelucano lume
di una barca che passa e un canto:
Harry Lime . . . che annotta nell'ascolto.

I don't know what memory you sing
now that I hold in my hands
the cold saltwater rain
and in my eyes the sign of clear currents glistens.
For us it's sorrow that dissolves the face,
my airy image, and for the one who is
searching for you, in a dream there is
a barge passing by in predawn light and a song:
Harry Lime . . . that darkens as he listens.

Liberazione

Vi saranno ancora giorni mùtili
in cui la mano cercherà la mano
per una carità che ci sospinga
alla quiete
le spalle contro il muro di casa
parlottando nella sera
con esperienza patita
e un fuoco fatuo negli occhi.

Giorni in cui non sarà facile
comprenderci
per un giuoco improvviso del sangue
o per il lamento della fame
o per il grido dell'ira.
Ci nutriremo della nostra pazienza.

Come bandiere ammainate
attenderemo un giorno di sole
per rifiorire sulle strade e andare
conserti alle nostre speranze
verso la guancia di Dio.

Civitavecchia 1951

Liberation

There will still be mutilated days
when the hand goes searching for the hand
out of a compassion that impels us
toward stillness
backs against the wall of the house
talking quietly in the evening
with haggard experience
and a will-o'-the-wisp in the eyes.

Days when it will not be easy
to understand each other
because of a sudden movement of the blood
or the groan of hunger
or the cry of rage.
We will feed ourselves upon our patience.

Like lowered flags
we'll wait for a sunny day
to blossom on the avenues and go
intertwined in our hopes
toward the cheek of God.

Civitavecchia, 1951

Limpida notte

Benedici la mia sera, Signore, la mano è quieta,
e se le vene furono ebbre d'altri piaceri
ed il sentiero salii dell'illusione,
ora ho lo sguardo velato del morente.
— Obliata esistenza, t'appaci sulle foglie immobili
e plana sul creato il tepore delle tue pupille;
e me, che strinsi i frutti della vita e risi,
straniero, me piega il tuo sereno,
la vita dei tuoi occhi, Signore.

Benedici la mia sera, Signore: nei solchi
cade la dolce semente, la tua misericordia,
e un fermo lago di rose è fiorito dal tuo amore
e per la tua bontà brilla il sole intenerito.
Se guardo il tuo viso arde in me la pace
e sono triste, Signore, se pur nelle attorte voglie
fluì, più tenera dell'amore,
la dolcezza della veniente sera.

Benedici la mia sera, Signore.
Sarò silente, nelle tue mani,
e consenziente alla morte pia;
il mio volere, torbido, s'accosterà al tuo seno
simile al bimbo greve di sonno
reclinante il capo nel grembo della madre.
Benedici, Signore: lento discende il tuo riposo
sulle curve rame che palpitano
come gola di passero dormente.

Clear Night

Bless my evening, Lord, my hand is calm,
and if my veins were drunk on other pleasures
and I climbed up the pathway of illusion,
now I have the veiled gaze of the dying.
—Forgotten existence, you're appeased on the still leaves
and the warmth of your pupils glides over creation;
and me, who squeezed the fruits of life and laughed,
a foreigner, your starry sky subdues me,
the life of your eyes, O Lord.

Bless my evening, Lord: into the furrows
falls the sweet seed, your mercy, and a still
lake of roses is flowering from your love
and through your kindness shines the softened sun.
If I look upon your face peace burns within me
and I am sad, Lord, even if in my twisted cravings
there flowed, more tender than love,
the sweetness of the coming evening.

Bless my evening, Lord.
I will be silent, in your hands,
and acquiesce in charitable death;
my will, so troubled, will approach your breast
like a little child heavy with sleep
resting his head upon his mother's lap.
Bless, Lord: slowly your repose descends
on the bowed branches that are trembling like
the throat of a sleeping sparrow.

Limpida notte salirà a vanire la vita
in te s'affiocherà la solitudine dei giorni
come, in tempo radioso, un aperto mattino.

Clear night will rise to spirit life away
in you the solitude of days will dim
like the dawn unfolding in bright weather.

Che nel sangue pulsasse . . .

Che nel sangue pulsasse l'aliseo buono
sapevo, e pensavo ch'ogni turbamento
nasceva ad ogni scalo voluto, per un cielo
che non sarebbe stato più mio;
per un fantasticare di albe tra le case
dai gerani aperti al maestrale;
che il pescatore conduceva a mano
tra le fitte favole del mare,
e ciuffi d'agave e i pini tremuli
nella calura . . .
                    Una pena ch'io doveva
trasportare da camera a camera,
da un sogno ad altro sogno
come un fardello prezioso al sillabare
intimo del cuore.
TIRESIA DIXIT

That the Good Trade Wind . . .

That the good trade wind pounded in the blood
I knew, and thought that every restlessness
was born in every sought-for port of call,
for a sky that would be mine no longer;
for a daydream of dawns between the houses
with geraniums open to the mistral;
that it led the fisherman by the hand
between the close-packed fables of the sea,
and clumps of agave plants and tremulous pines
in the oppressive heat . . .
                                        A punishment,
a pain I had to bear from room to room,
carry from one dream to another dream
like a precious burden to be spelled out
close within the heart.
                                        TIRESIA DIXIT

Dicebant mihi sodales . . .

A Édith Piaf

Donando qualche radura ai silenzi,
un sussurro.
Ho conosciuto il giorno
dagli immensi risvegli, il passo
pesante del dolore. Ché,
se ti piega il vento, freme
e trascolora il bosco:
da un sussultare di sillabe fiorisci.

La valle s'inebria al cuore
che batte
e si rinchiude, oro di tutti i tramonti,
tra le palpebre . . .

Dicebant mihi sodales . . .

Dicebant Mihi Sodales . . .

To Édith Piaf

Giving a clearing to the silences,
a whisper.
I have known the day
by its immense awakenings, the heavy
step of pain. Because,
if the wind bends you over, the forest
quivers and fades:
you flower from a startle of syllables.

The valley's intoxicated by the heart
that beats
and closes itself up, gold of all the sunsets,
between the eyelids . . .

Dicebant mihi sodales . . .

Tentazione e controtentazione (1951)

I

Poiché non credo esattamente
all'amore eroico che nutre la terra,
(uccelli neri ornano il cielo sui boulevards
e indugiano nel segreto dei capitelli)
sapendo che i primitivi affetti
germogliano dal cuore e che il Male
è la sorte del Bene lasciato inaridire
io associo, deliberatamente,
ogni tua amarezza alla mia vanità.

Preso dallo stupore, avvinto dal genuino candore
che sorregge in questa sua essenza ogni piano malvagio,
ma forte della mia incomparabile speranza,
arrischio insinuanti parole
conformate alla sua malagrazia:

Io non so quando Mosé ha scagliato le sue tavole
sulle guglie di Roma o perché mai Rut
non ha lasciato ad altri il suo campo da spigolare
(più vaste ali vogliono a fianco dell'anima).
Io non so la noia che ti si snoda accanto
quando odi riecheggiare il SUO NOME
nel vuoto delle asciutte cisterne,
non so la spaventosa scena
che sarà diffusa domani dai giornali.

Temptation and Countertemptation (1951)

I

Because I don't exactly believe in
the heroic love that nourishes the earth
(black birds adorn the sky over boulevards
and secretly loiter on column capitals),
knowing that the primitive affections
sprout from the heart and that Evil is
the destiny of Good that's left to wither
I associate, deliberately,
all your bitterness with my vanity.

Seized with amazement, struck by the genuine innocence
that supports in its essence every malevolent plan,
but strong in my incomparable hope,
I take the risk of insinuating words
well adapted to its lack of grace:

I don't know when Moses hurled his Tables
onto the spires of Rome or why Ruth didn't
leave the gleaning of her field to others
(they want wider wings at the spirit's side).
I don't know the ennui that comes near you
when you hear HIS NAME reechoing
in the emptiness of dried-up cisterns,
I don't know the frightful scene that will
be circulated in tomorrow's papers.

Io ascolto il Puro Essere, il Bello Elementare
che soffia implacato nell'argilla.

II

Se vuoi districare quelle presenze
che mi esiliano dalla Tua nudità,
Vento memorabile sulle piazze di Sodoma e Gomorra;
se vuoi avvertire Lot che separi
nel bianco torpore dell'atrio della sua casa
le violenze insidiose dai teneri approcci;
se non ho da cogliere, vanamente, un presentimento,
con lunghi spasimi del cuore,
da questo Tuo soffiare livido
che dilata e incide l'orizzonte;
se tutto è una coagulata parvenza che decresce:
Signore, perché mai mi stupisce
il Tuo venire inosservato dalla fonte dell'amore?

(Ti tengo, BEATITUDINE, nel verde di questo ebbro
passaggio
ti tengo nella fragilità del mio gaudio
ti tengo e ti indosso serica camicia tepente).

III

Poiché ancora ci seduce l'elogio compiacente
ed ogni nostra rispondenza è ferita dalla noia,
poiché la nostra vanità vorrebbe, precorsa ai Tuoi occhi,
l'edificazione eterna di un più lieto futuro,
poiché ogni inutile parola ci attarda l'aurora

I listen to the Pure Being, the Elemental Beauty
that whispers unrelentingly in the clay.

II

If you wish to disentangle those
presences that exile me from Your nakedness,
a memorable Wind upon the squares of Sodom and Gomorrah;
if you wish to warn Lot to distinguish
in blank numbness at the entrance of his house
insidious assaults from soft approaches;
if I do not have to grasp, in vain, a presentiment,
with long pangs of the heart,
of Your livid breathing
that expands and incises the horizon;
if all is a curdled diminishing apparition:
Lord, why am I astonished
by Your arriving unseen from the fountainhead of love?

(I hold you, BLESSEDNESS, in the greenery of this drunken
 passage
I hold you in the fragility of my joy
I hold you and I wear you, warm silky shirt.)

III

Since we are still seduced by complaisant praise
and all of our conforming is injured by ennui,
since our vanity would like, anticipated by Your eyes,
the eternal construction of a happier future,
since every useless word delays the dawn for us

e un cumulo di scorie è nelle sillabe alternate,
poiché geometrizziamo i canoni dell'obbedienza
e limitiamo le ampiezze massime dell'umiltà,
noi che ostentiamo atti poco aperti ad ogni vigore
e che ci intenerisce anche la più giusta condanna,
noi che ci assale il dubbio vacuo della Tua esistenza,
che ci storna e ci trascina anche il più ingenuo profeta,
noi, abissale agonia della calma celestiale,
noi, anime in prova, noi Tua creta che rifiati,
noi Ti preghiamo per il vigore della vita universa
entro la zolla che il Tuo impeto ricupera immortale,
noi Ti preghiamo per la pietà che il Tuo amore disasconde,
noi Ti preghiamo per la certezza ultima dei trapassi.

IV

Di là dai Grandi Occhi scrutammo enigmi inestricati,
il silenzio enunciato nell'incavo delle labbra
dalle attive vocali; ma ora che il nostro sangue
ammulina i ritmi e disdegna l'onnipresente sopore,
il respiro dei mondi regge te stessa, anima mia,
e rigenera gli andamenti, sciolti dalle tenebre, ai volumi.

and there is a heap of slag in alternate syllables,
since we geometrize the canons of obedience
and limit the maximum ranges of humility,
we who flaunt scarcely open actions with every vigor
and are also moved by the most deserved condemnation,
we who are seized with empty doubts of Your existence
diverted and carried away by even the most foolish prophet,
we, bottomless anguish of celestial tranquility,
we, souls that are on trial, we Your clay that You breathe,
we pray to You for the strength of universal life
within the sod Your impetus restores to immortality,
we pray to You for the mercy that Your love discloses,
we pray to You for the final certainty of the passings.

IV

Beyond the Great Eyes we peer at unpenetrated enigmas,
the silence enunciated in the cavity of the lips
by active vowels; but now that this blood of ours is whirling
the rhythms and disdaining the omnipresent drowsiness,
the breath of all the worlds supports even you, my soul,
and regenerates the movements of the spheres, loosed from
the dark.

Poesie del '53

I

Ora tutto questo da affrontare.

Non ci chiesero il perdono
quando ci destammo entro il chiuso,
nel vivo del bersaglio,
tra il rischio inconsueto del reale
e il terrore che è sbandata solitudine.
Non calmarono in noi l'acceso evento dell'ira,
ci impartirono invece la lezione del guadagno
e dissero morte, l'ombra della madre,
una pausa compiaciuta della vita.

Ora il folle gioco penetra ovunque
nel silenzio e nel parlare aperto,
misura ogni nostra solitudine,
ci sorprende furtivo alle calcagna,
galleggia suasivo nel sangue dei defunti
destinato oramai a quello di noi vivi.
Noi da voi ereditiamo l'imboscata del dubbio
che sigla la sintassi del mondo.

Ora tutto questo da affrontare
senza tregua
a conclusione di un'era abnorme
a confino della tenebra.

Gennaio 1953

Poems of ’53

I

Now all of this to confront.

They didn’t ask our pardon
when we awakened inside the enclosure,
in the bull’s-eye of the target,
between the unusual danger of the real
and the terror that is isolated solitude.
They didn’t calm the rage that burned inside us,
but instead they passed the lesson of profit on to us
and spoke of death, the shadow of the mother,
a complacent interruption of this life.

Now the mad game penetrates everywhere
in silence and in speaking openly,
measuring our every loneliness,
catching us in secret by the heels,
floating winningly in the blood of the deceased
now headed for that of us who are still alive.
From you we inherit the ambush of doubt
that initials the syntax of the world.

Now all of this to confront
without a truce
at the conclusion of an abnormal time
in the confines of the dark.

January 1953

II

Il vento, il vento che l'incrina muta il tuo passo.
La sera in fermo cielo ora trascorre,
d'una prismatica storia disegna l'orma
e su una cupa lastra slabbrata
un'ombra lusinga senza stupore.

E dunque volevamo essere da sempre
alla speranza
e dunque al bacio della notte
e dunque gioia, a specchio capovolta.

A maturare il gioco in gran silenzio,
e il vento,
il vento un vuoto mostruosamente inciso,
il vento cova inquieto e pare immoto
al limite interrotto di parole.

Febbraio 1953

II

The wind, the wind that cracks it changes your stride.
Evening elapses now in a steady sky,
sketching the mark of a prismatic story
and on a chipped slab of dark stone
a shadow entices without wonder.

And then we wished to be eternally
in hopefulness
and then in the kiss of night
and then joy, inverted in a mirror.

Developing the game in a great silence,
and the wind,
the wind a monstrously etched emptiness,
the wind broods anxiously and seems unmoving
at the broken boundary of words.

Febbraio 1953

da L'ALLELUJA (1952)

from THE ALLELUIA (1952)

Signore, il muro è cresciuto

per Ezra Pound

Come sarà il verde delle querce?
Davanti a casa mia v'era un filare di querce,
capelli verdi
verde-cielo dopo che tramonta il sole:
non le ho più vedute.
Da cinque anni non vedo il verde delle querce,
da cinque anni, Signore,
ho gli occhi grigi
da cinque anni vedo solo pietre
pietre
e non colgo — con un battito d'ali nel cuore
— i primi bisbigli dell'alba tra le foglie;
non colgo che pietre
da cinque anni. Ho gli occhi grigi
dal troppo fissare le pietre.

Signore, il muro è cresciuto e vedo solo il cielo,
le quercie son sepolte nel mio cuore;
son cresciuti i muri
e gli occhi guardano il cielo,
il Tuo vestito verde come il cielo
dopo ch'è tramontato il sole.
Guarderò il cielo Signore;
Signore, se vuoi,
gli occhi diverranno verdi
come il cielo
(dopo ch'è tramontato il sole).

Lord, the Wall Has Risen

for Ezra Pound

How will the green of the oak trees be?
In front of my house there was a row of oak trees,
green-haired
sky-green after the the sun goes down:
I don't see them anymore.
For five years I haven't seen the green of the oak trees.
For five years, Lord,
I've had gray eyes
for five years I've seen only rocks
rocks
and I don't gather—with a flutter of wings in my heart
—the first murmurings of dawn between the leaves.
I've gathered only rocks
for five years. I have gray eyes
from too much staring at rocks.

Lord, the wall has risen and all I see is the sky,
the oak trees are all buried in my heart.
The walls have risen
and my eyes look at the sky,
the green of your garments, green as the sky
after the sun has gone down.
I'll look at the sky, Lord;
Lord, if you desire,
my eyes will turn green
like the sky
(after the sun has gone down).

Dopo ch'è tramontato il sole
io vedrò Te e il verde delle querce.
Ma come saranno i verdi capelli delle querce?

After the sun has gone down
I'll see You and the green of the oak trees.
But how will the green hair of the oak trees be?

Città

Vidi brillare le fiammelle ai ceri,
nella Cattedrale:
accanto la riviera dei passi e case,
ragazze succinte alla finestra.
Sui passi,
silenzïose,
non trapelava la luce,
non trapela il canto.
Come un fiume invernale, raggelato,
stanno quiete le case
ad ascoltare il rombo
delle automobili . . . Le mani
portano al volto l'illusione.

Sul corso stormivano le foglie
tra le dita vaporose della sera.
Stormivano anni sepolti
luce di stelle. Le ragazze,
inchiodata la finestra,
dilagarono sulla via:
nudi fanali
tra un blocco e l'altro di case.

Una dopo l'altra vanirono le fiamme,
l'ultima si spense: aurore
sorgevano di sangue, e andavano
soffocando la speranza delle strade,
le ragazze molli. Il coro,

City

I saw the little flames of candles shining,
in the Cathedral:
close to the coast of passageways and houses,
half-naked girls inside the window.
Along the passageways,
silent,
no light leaked through,
no song leaks through.
Like a winter river, frozen over,
houses are keeping still
to listen to the rumble
of automobiles . . . The hands
carry the illusion to the face.

The leaves were rustling on the avenue
between the wispy fingers of the evening.
Buried years were rustling
starlight. The young girls,
the window nailed shut,
flooded the street:
bare lights
between one block of houses and the other.

The flames all went out one after the other,
the last one died away: dawns
rose up full of blood, and went about
smothering the hope of the avenues,
the soft girls. The choir,

felpato
dalla sacrestia,
già bisbigliava nella notte, fuori:

Quidquid latet, apparebit.

treading
softly from the sacristy,
already whispered in the night, outside:

Quidquid latet, apparebit.

Il fiume

per Gherardo del Colle

Perché so che il tempo è sempre il tempo
e lo spazio è sempre e solo lo spazio
e ciò ch'è attuale lo è per una volta sola
T. S. Eliot, *Ash Wednesday*

Il crepuscolo

I

Donne io vidi
chinarsi sulle prode
ad ascoltare il fiume.
Donne io vidi quando il cielo è verde
prone sulle mie labbra
il cielo giocava sulle carni ingnude
giallo e verde il cielo
l'alto canneto oscillava.
        Io vidi in sogno i loro sogni
lacrime e riso
stanchi
sul fuggitivo ansito del fiume
ché di tante speranze . . .
        Una
sera in cui la dolce luna
        si fendeva nel seno
        del desiderio
in cui la dolce luna
flautava nel sangue
sotterraneo
e vaniva il tuo lamento autunnale
sulla mia gola canora, appena
più alta del frusciante fiume

The River

for Gherardo del Colle

Because I know that time is always time
and place is always and only place
and what is actual is actual only for one time
T. S. Eliot, *Ash Wednesday*

The Twilight

I

Women I saw
bending over the banks
to listen to the river.
Women I saw when the sky is green
prone on my lips
the sky was playing on their naked flesh
the yellow and green sky
the tall cane-brakes were swaying.
    In a dream I saw their dreams
tears and laughter
weary
on the runaway panting of the river
because of so many hopes . . .
    One
evening when the sweet moon
    split itself on the breast
    of desire
when the sweet moon
fluted in the hidden
blood
and your autumn lamentation disappeared
on my singing throat, scarcely
higher than the murmuring river

tra l'alte foglie: io vidi
                    e se n'andava
dondolando l'ànche nel
pigro bagno di luna
forte l'ombra sul fiume
e risaliva alla sorgente.

II

Donne io vidi
e il tempo è il tempo
ma una ne vidi
cadere e poi rialzarsi
ineffabile
varcare i limiti del tempo
una che ne vidi
e le conobbi tutte, e il riso
che ancora echeggia alle mie spalle

Et alors je pense à ton Désir
Natanaele
a questa amara saliva
a questo rigurgito d'alghe
viscide e amare
che il fiume porge alla mia sete

    E già mi volti le spalle
anche tu
aureo giglio di latta

e mi trascina prigioniero il fiume
    anche tu
    prigioniero
e mi trascina.

amid the high leaves: I saw
                                        and she went away
swinging her hips in
the lazy bath of the moon
the shadow strong on the river
and it returned to the source.

II

Women I saw
and time is time
but one of them I saw
fall and pick herself up
ineffable
crossing the limits of time
one of them that I saw
and I knew them all, and the laughter
that I can still hear echoing behind me

Et alors je pense à ton Désir
Natanaele
in this bitter saliva
in this regurgitation of slimy
and bitter algae
that the river offers to my thirst

      And already you turn your back on me
you too
golden tin lily

and the river pulls me along a prisoner
      you too
      prisoner
and it pulls me along.

September

I

Il fiume corre alla sua pace
lo dice il falco remigante e cieco
alto nel sole lontanante,
lo dice il cielo
vela protesa alle partenze
        e noi, sfogliati nelle sale d'aspetto
        e noi, gonfi di scorie

poi subito i treni, che vanno
e l'ultimo rondò dei calabroni
che vanno
                gli occhi
e la memoria s'inselvan di fantàsime venienti
incontro
a le prime tremule nebbie, i ricordi:

ciò che non si dice ancora
per pietà, sullo squallido viale
ai primi amori con le foglie.

II

Ed, ecco, passano fruscianti
tante morti nel cielo e un primo
candore di nubi
fuscelli delle valli mietute
        i morti cieli
i bimbi che gridano dal limbo

September

I

The river runs to its peace
so says the falcon beating his wings and blind
high in the distant sun,
so says the sky
sail stretched out for departure
        and we, stripped down in waiting rooms
        and we, swollen with waste

then right away the trains, that go
and the final rondo of the hornets
that go
                the eyes
and the memory take to the woods of apparitions
coming
to meet the first tremulous hazes, recollections:

that which is not yet said
out of pity, on the seedy avenue
to the first loves with the leaves.

II

And, here, they pass by rustling
so many dead in the sky and a first
splendor of clouds
twigs of the harvested valleys
        the dead skies
the babies who cry out from limbo

le ciniche risate dei condoms
le voci
sfioranti le predate curve dei seni
le prime vendemmie dei naufraghi
sul tepido lido ammainato
        ove ogni corpo
        ha lasciato:
le dolci mani illuse
il tenero segno delle ànche doloranti
il labirinto dei desideri
gli amori inceneriti
dall'ardente stagione,
ove tutto ciò ch'è umano
ha la sua tomba fluente
e rifluente negli anni
che saranno
                    « ahimé
tutto il rossetto s'è sfatto
sulle tue labbra », « e tu credi
ch'io possa credere ancora » ,
« questa non è l'ora
d'Ofelia . . . » , « il gusto
che hai
di sorridere in un'ora come questa! »

Cresce la voce azzurra
cresce la mano fresca
assottigliando i limiti

Il fiume corre alla sua pace.

the cynical cackling of condoms
the voices
grazing the plundered curves of breasts
the first harvests of shipwrecks
on the lukewarm flag-lowered shore
        where every body
        has left behind:
the gentle deluded hands
the tender token of the aching hips
the labyrinth of desires
the loves incinerated
by the blazing season,
where all that is human
has its tomb flowing
and reflowing in the years
that will be
                "sad to say
all the lipstick's worn away
from your lips," "and you believe
that I can still believe,"
"this is not the age
of Ophelia . . . ," "what zest
you have
that you can smile in a time like this!"

The blue voice rises
the cool hand rises
blurring the boundaries

The river runs to its peace.

III

E allora, Ennio, trai
dalla tasca il giornale e siedi

« LE PRIME PIOGGE »

siedi con i tuoi pochi capelli
con il tuo sesso trafitto
dalle stagioni

il fiume corre alla sua pace
e il sangue trepido lambe
        i ricordi
tutto vapora e più limpido
corre alla sua pace

e più limpida canta la sua pace
e sul canto s'alza la luna
i richiami del Cacciatore
s'alza la luna pregna di settembre
oh s'alza la luna

all time is unredeemable.

III

And then, Ennio, pull
the newspaper from your pocket and sit down

"EARLY RAINS"

sit down with your few hairs
with your sex pierced
by the seasons

the river runs to its peace
and the anxious blood grazes
        memories
everything evaporates and more clearly
runs to its peace

and more clearly sings its peace
and on the song the moon rises
the Hunter's calls
the September full moon rises
oh the moon rises

all time is unredeemable.

Le strade

Le corps est la baraque où notre existence est campée
Joubert

I

« Beaux gars, beaux gars! »
Il sasso
cade nella palude;
tocca, la mano, gli angoli più infermi. Io salgo,
nel profumo sbiadito dei licheni,
il paradiso dei consunti gradini.
La luce rosa mi divora.

Mon pays est Paris: dal vicolo
bruisce il mondo: è sulle scale,
sui davanzali a ferire i gerani;
a rivoltare fritture di pesce
sotto i porticati
vorticati dai cittadini del mare.
Consolazione delle lampade rosa
e viola, la sera è sul selciato
umido per lo scirocco.
Non v'è più nulla da dare.
Le salette inaridiscono
simili a fiori di vetro
nel pigro cielo dei camerieri. I trams
(la notte di seta arrota i denti) vanno
e vengono, l'ultime corse ai capilinea:
un ragioniere porta la sua stanca passione
a sfiorire
tra i primi buffi oleosi di erba,
di là dalla luce. (*Mea culpa*, *mea*
culpa) una mosca prigioniera ronza

The Roads

Le corps est la baraque où notre existence est campée
Joubert

I

"*Beaux gars, beaux gars!*"
The stone
falls into the swamp;
it touches, the hand, the more unhealthy corners. I ascend,
in the faded fragrance of the lichens,
the paradise of wornout steps.
The rose light swallows me.

Mon pays est Paris: from the alley
the world is rustling: it's on the stairs,
on the windowsills to wound the geraniums;
to turn the frying fish over
under those bustling
porticos of the citizens of the sea.
Consolation of the violet and rose
lamps, the evening is on the cobblestones
damp from the scirocco.
There's nothing left to give there.
The little rooms grow dry
like flowers made of glass
in the waiters' sluggish sky. The trams
(the silken night grinds its teeth) are going
and coming, the last runs to the end of the line:
an accountant's carrying his tired passion
to wither
amid the first oleaginous breaths of grass,
beyond the light. (*Mea culpa, mea
culpa*) a trapped fly is buzzing away

nell'acidula ombra di una chiesa.

Le strade distendono le membra in croce
nel sonno ventilato dalla polvere.

Poi viene la morte e s'adagia
tra me e lei. Ha le labbra rosse
e guance pallide di cipria. « Sai?
— mi dice — sono stanca. Su e giù,
terribilmente stanca . . . », « Buona sera »,
dico, e m'accompagna
il puzzo di saliva dei suoi seni.

II

La chair est triste, hélas! Non hai più voce
che torni a popolare di fantasmi
l'angoscia di questo sole. Il cane
purulento beve un dito d'ombra
lungo i palazzi disumani.
Qual samaritano porge
acque lustrali alla mia sete? Un cane,
dissepolto dal deserto bianco
del meriggio,
ossa accecanti, occhio feroce, corre
nei miei sangui; corre
attorno all'ampia piazza: il muro è chiuso,
anela la fuga per i verdi prati,
il naso puntato al tordo che saetta,
fresco di note, tra i giunchi, verso il cielo. . . .
Hélas! un cerchio chiude la passione
nella piazza cieca. — *A trois heures*
le sang bouillonne, — dicevo al cameriere

in the acidic shadow of a church.

The roads stretch out their limbs upon a cross
in a sleep ventilated by the dust.

Then death comes and stretches out
between me and her. She has red lips
and cheeks white with powder. "Do you know?"
she says to me, "I'm tired. Up and down,
terribly tired . . ." "Good evening,"
I say, and the stink
of spittle from her breasts comes along with me.

II

La chair est triste, hélas! You do not have
the voice left to come back and populate
the anguish of this sun with ghosts. The purulent
dog is drinking up a finger of shadow
beside the inhuman palazzos.
What Samaritan extends
some gleaming water for my thirst? A dog,
disinterred from the white midday
desert,
bones blinding, eyes ferocious, is running
in my veins; is running
all around the spacious square: the wall is closed,
he's yearning to take off for the green fields,
nose pointing at the thrush that's darting past,
pouring out notes, amid the reeds, toward the sky. . . .
Hélas! a circle's closed around his pain
there in the blocked-up square. —*A trois heures
le sang bouillonne*, I said to the waiter

sulla soglia del bar. Il mondo
vaporava il suo sudore,
il sudore di noi.
Il sudore, o Cristo benedetto,
che piega le ginocchia . . .
Il sudore che piega le ginocchia,
l'anima che piega le ginocchia.

Nessun organetto tenta la mia voce, ché,
mi dicevo, se sorgesse un filo
di voce,
uno stelo d'erba nel ricordo,
potrei fuggire questa piazza deserta,
il forno crematorio della mia anima.

Un cane corre su di un dito d'ombra.
La piazza è in ogni dove. È giunta,
portando l'anche molle, — *Oh, chéri*!
— diritta sul mio cuore.

III

Batto ai vetri delle case. Batto
ai vetri delle case. Il sangue
fiorisce sulla gronda, sale
al vento dei comignoli.
        Un sonno torpido
per i sentieri dell'alba,
la città rossa sbadiglia
nel solco lutulento delle carraie.

Batto, cieca falena, ai vetri
del deserto; batto

in the doorway of the cafe. The world
evaporated his sweat,
our sweat.
The sweat, O blessed Christ,
that bends the knees . . .
The sweat that bends the knees,
the soul that bends the knees.

No barrel organ tempts my voice, because
I told myself, if a wisp of voice
arose,
a blade of grass here in my memory,
I could escape this deserted square,
the crematory furnace of my soul.

A dog is running on a finger of shadow.
The square is everywhere. It has arrived,
carrying its soft hips, —*Oh, chéri*!
—right onto my heart.

III

I knock at the windows of the houses. I knock
at the windows of the houses. Blood
blossoms on the eaves, it rises
to the wind of the chimneys.
        A sluggish slumber
along the paths of dawn,
the red city yawns
in the muddy furrow of the wagon roads.

I knock, blind moth, at the windows
of the desert; I knock

alle sinuose morti bianche,
e in sillabe il lamento,
il mio stupore,
il perché
di questo giallo deserto . . . (Fra i lini
caldi: il sangue irrompe a cateratte
nel ruvido alveo delle vene,
a crear fiabe. Oh basta, basta! Oh questa
voglia terribile! Piagnucola la voce
nel muschioso abisso
rapito ai giorni e spolpato, dopo,
e in secca tra gli aridi tronchi delle cosce. I lini
caldi, il sudore . . .).
Oltre la nebbia è nato il Bambino.
È nato il Redentore! Un poco
di verde nel ricordo, un po'
di Pan e cronachette di sampogna
sotto le stelle . . . e, via sul vento! A brani, a filacce,
la fresca notte, silenziosa e santa . . .
È morto il Redentore.
Il Bambino s'è messo a camminare sul vento,
sul vento delle sue parole.

Sul letto muoiono le foglie,
le morte foglie. Sul letto
giace la città: le strade morte,
i palazzi dalle pàlpebre abbassate
pudibondi e ipocriti; le morte bocche
spalancate nel récere i morti paradisi.
Sul letto
fluttua il rosso sangue dei lampioni.

Il vento ara il sale della notte.

at the tortuous white deaths,
and in syllables the lament,
my astonishment,
the why
of this yellow desert . . . (Between the hot
linens: blood surges into cataracts
in the rough riverbed of the veins,
to engender fables. Oh, enough, enough! Oh, this
terrible craving! The voice is whispering
in the musky abyss
kidnapped for days and stripped clean, afterwards,
and in drought between the arid trunks of thighs. The hot
linens, the sweat . . .).
Beyond the mist the Holy Child is born.
The Redeemer is born! A bit
of green in the memory, a bit
of Pan and little chronicles of bagpipes
under the stars . . . and, away on the wind! In scraps, in shreds,
the cool night, silent and holy . . .
The Redeemer is dead.
The Holy Child set out upon the wind,
on the wind of his words.

The leaves die on the bed,
the dead leaves. On the bed
the city lies: the dead roads,
the prudish and hypocritical apartment
buildings with lowered eyelids; the dead mouths
wide open as they vomit dead paradises.
On the bed
the red blood of the streetlights fluctuates.

The wind is plowing the salt of the night.

Un dono troppo caro

per il poeta amico Angelo Barile

I

Era sogno la notte
nell'inconscio bagliore del sonno,
un porto. Ed era
dolce seguire gl'istinti
che al tutto sospingeva il ricordo
presente: ed era l'ineffabile,
raccolto e trasformato in viaggi
dell'innocenza al sempre,
su la pupilla murata dell'esistenza.

Un dono troppo caro.

E vivere per ciò che è fuori? Cadere
nel pallore desertico del giorno:
la voce disperata dei selciati
udii librarsi, straniera, dal mio petto
e, dalla notte, dilungarsi,
tra le case spente, illusi passi;
trasalire gli alberi.
E più il sole saliva nel cielo
più i silenzi nebbiosi del pensiero
cagliavano nell'ombre
raccolte sul deserto.

Ciò che avanza dai perduti lidi
nel ricordo, lagrima, s'apprende
e non sai . . .

A Gift Too Dear

for my poet friend Angelo Barile

I

Night was a dream
in the unconscious glow of sleep,
a port. And it was
sweet to follow the instincts
that the present recollection impelled
to the all: and it was the ineffable,
collected and transformed in voyages
of innocence to forever,
on the walled-up pupil of existence.

A gift too dear.

And to live for what's outside? To fall
into the desert pallor of the day:
I heard the desperate voice of the cobblestones
breaking free, a stranger, from my chest
and, by night, deluded footsteps
lingering among the extinguished houses;
the trees giving a start.
And the more the sun rose in the sky
the more the misty silences of thought
curdled into shadows
collected on the desert.

That which advances from lost shores
in recollection, weeps, takes hold
and you don't know . . .

II

Esistono i campanili
dalle voci d'argento
volteggiati dai corvi:
le quattro stagioni
sono un vicolo cieco.

III

L'oceano è un vicolo cieco.
Il giorno è un vicolo cieco.
Bisogna perdersi,
il costato trafitto
dalla fugace speranza delle rondini.

La tua voce, o Signore!
la tua voce suadente,
nuda come il nostro sonno:
la tua voce che romba
sotto la fragile crosta dei giorni,
che spazia sopra le nostre esistenza
e ci abbandona, vuoti, sugli argini!
La tua voce squallida come ossa
(i nostri sogni plasmammo
sulle tua ossa), o voce vera
nei fili telefonici,
sulle antenne tremanti della radio,
abbandonata al flusso delle maree,
all'impeto delle stagioni
e risorgente in noi,

II

There are belltowers
with voices of silver
circled by ravens:
the four seasons
are a blind alley.

III

The ocean is a blind alley.
The day is a blind alley.
We have to lose ourselves,
side pierced
by the fleeting hope of swallows.

Your voice, O Lord!
your persuasive voice,
naked as our sleep:
your voice that rumbles
underneath the brittle crust of days,
expatiating over our existence,
and abandons us, hollowed, on embankments!
Your voice as dismal as bones
(we molded our dreams
on your bones), O real voice
in telephone wires,
on quivering radio antennas,
abandoned to the flow of tides,
to the impetus of the seasons
and resurgent in us,

forza cieca . . . ! Lontano
i campanili: bisogna
vivere, bisogna
perdersi.

IV

Oltre il velo della pioggia
s'ode il battito lento
delle vene:

Tra le foglie verdi delle querci
fendono la bruma
soprascarpe di gomma e queruli
campanelli: i nasi contro i vetri
dei bar, nudi.
Una luce, non Tua,
ci trapassa dalle insegne. Lei
sollevò gli occhi, attenta: sentiva
l'unica speranza allontanarsi . . .

Improvvisamente rimasta
tra le corolle sporche dei guanciali,
e già fuggiva sui binari morti del sangue
il suo sospiro, lontano,
nella memoria . . . Oggi,
sotto gli ombrelli, gli uomini
si tendono le mani

— Ah, Signore, abbiamo goduto
una meravigliosa sconfitta!

blind force . . . ! Belltowers
far away: we have to live,
we have to lose
ourselves.

IV

Beyond the veil of rain
we hear the slow beating
of the veins:

Amid the green leaves hanging from oak trees
rubber galoshes
and querulous bells are cutting through
the mist: noses pressed against the glass
of cafés, naked.
A light, not Yours,
pierces us from their neon signs. She
raised her eyes, attentive: she could sense
the only hope distancing itself . . .

Left all at once
among the soiled corollas of the pillows,
and her sigh already escaped on the dead tracks
of the blood, far away,
in my memory . . . Today,
under their umbrellas, the men
hold out their hands

—Ah, Lord, we have enjoyed
a marvelous defeat!

— Buon giorno
  Buona sera

Ahimè, buona notte.

V

O giorno, effimera coscienza di noi!
Non sappiamo altro.
Solo questo cielo senza gridi, eterno.
Tu, ala gravida di gioie,
batti sullo stagno
vibrandolo d'interminabili echi
ancestrali: un profumo di nubi
e alberi
e, di pupilla in pupilla, ad acquitrini
ove algida sboccia
un'antica speranza di giorni . . .

Frangere il velo taciturno
che di noi conchiude l'esistenza
in una gelida ira!

Le sublimi orchidee sfrondi
ed iridi fugaci
esprimi in sillabe, ma il sonno,
ov'alitano i miti, è sempre
al di là del tuo esilio, o giorno,
giorno delle colline brulle
invano irrigate dal pianto di Prometeo,
giorno verde nel fango della strada!

—Good morning
Good evening

Alas, good night.

V

O day, ephemeral consciousness for us!
We don't know any other.
Only this sky without a cry, eternal.
You, wing pregnant with joys,
beat upon the pond
making it vibrate with interminable
ancestral echoes: a perfume of clouds
and trees
and, from pupil to pupil, to the marshes
where cold as ice
there blossoms an old-fashioned hope of days . . .

Oh, to shatter the taciturn veil
that brings existence to an end for us
in an icy rage!

You strip the sublime orchids of their leaves
and express the fleeting
irises in syllables, but sleep,
where the myths breathe, is always
beyond your banishment, O day,
day of the barren hills
watered in vain by the tears of Prometheus,
a green day in the mud of the roadway!

Fiore di carta

I

Pour ne plus songer à tes sanglots . . .
Tristan Derème

Colomba tu porti sotto l'ala
fumo di tigli nella sera
e sospirar di rivi sui silenzi
tremuli di luna.

(*Tu mi devi giurare;*
tu dimmi, dimmi quanto
amore posso sopportare).

Illusa.
La penombra casta
serpeggiava tra l'erbe
a rapirti la pupilla. E il sogno,
ch'io sentivo di là
querelare ormai la primavera
(*colomba, colomba!*) trasportava
il rude corso delle vene
a favolosi lidi.

Lo stame un grillo sega dei ricordi
nell'ampio respiro del meriggio
senza fate o gnomi.
S'erge rossa foresta,
fossile.

Paper Flower

I

Pour ne plus songer à tes sanglots . . .
Tristan Derème

Dove under your wing you carry
limewood smoke in the evening
and streams' breathing on quivering
silences of the moon.

(*You ought to swear*
to me; you tell me, tell me
how much love I can bear).

Deceived.
The chaste twilight
meandered amid the grasses
to ravish your eye. And the dream,
that I sensed over there
now lamenting the spring
(*dove, dove!*) carried
the rough course of the veins
to legendary shores.

A cricket saws the stamen of memories
in the expansive breath of noon
without fairies or gnomes.
A red forest rises,
petrified.

II

Ora mi giungi nel silenzio, gli occhi
impietriti dalla vita: un mito,
sabbia concreta di preistoria
tra le mie dita allentate: so.
Non devi pensare — querula amante,
— *evaporare devi i succhi amari*
della calda foresta . . . — Ma penso?
Fanciullo vecchio nel profumo
della tua parola (*vedi l'alba?*), tocco
ala di farfalla e guardo,
comparando l'anima nel fremito
il futuro al passato, polline sul dito
e, subito, un vento porta a intridersi di nebbie
questa vana speranza: come vedere l'alba?
Dal cosmo, stanco mulino,
s'alza un cachinno di riso

— Ah, ah, ah, quale alba? come,
come vedere l'alba?

II

Now you come to me in silence, with
eyes that are petrified by life: a myth,
the substantial prehistoric sand
slipping between my loosened fingers: I know.
You oughtn't to be thinking, querulous lover,
you ought to evaporate the bitter juices
of the steaming forest . . . But am I thinking?
An aged little child in the perfume
of your word (*do you see the dawn?*), I touch
the wing of a butterfly and I look
at the fluttering soul and make a comparison
between the past and future, pollen on
my finger, and then a wind brings the fog to befoul
this empty hope: how to see the dawn?
From the cosmos, exhausted mill,
I hear a hollow cackle rise

—Ha ha ha, what dawn? how,
how to see the dawn?

III

Nuit. Silence. O fin de chaque jour . . .
Luc Durtain

Monotona canzone.
Arcangeli piumati e con lorica
abbracciano Rimbaud sul ciglio della strada
intento ad ascoltar, sul murmure di schiavi,
il salmodiar di Dante e il dubbio
folle d'Amleto
in croce tra Sancio e l'Hidalgo,
ed io stanco d'essere un santo
dai piedi d'argilla:

dibattuti dal flusso eterno del fiume
che trascorre e rifluisce ai varchi:
sangue rappreso nel grido della Donna
a un Dio,
al vecchio paradiso
da cui fummo cacciati.

Ma la tua fiamma,
un palpito di luce sulle labbra oranti,
vacilla col mutar dei giorni.
Ogni sera una fiaba si spegne,
trascolorano vite
sulla nota gelida dell'*Ite*,
ite, missa est.

III

Nuit. Silence. O fin de chaque jour . . .
Luc Durtain

Monotonous song.
Archangels with feathers and wearing armor
embrace Rimbaud off at the side of the road
intent on hearing, over the murmurs of slaves,
Dante's psalm-singing and the mad
suspicion of Hamlet
on the cross between Sancho and the Hidalgo,
and I am so very tired of being a saint
with feet of clay:

troubled by the eternal flux of the river
that passes by and flows back to the gates:
clotted blood in the outcry of the Woman
to a God,
to the old paradise
from which we were cast out.

But your flame,
a fluttering of light on prayerful lips,
wavers with the changing of the days.
Every evening a fable dies away,
discoloring lives
on the icy note of *Ite,*
ite, missa est.

IV

Andante appassionato con ottoni e corde.
— *Ma io, io . . .* — , cantabile vento di contrada!
— *i seni colmi, il grembo, e sai . . .*
e tu non puoi abbandonar nel Lete
l'onirico sapore delle carni,
le vele schioccanti dei miei baci,
i baci . . .
e vene. — Cantano. — *Ma io, io!*
— Uccello che motteggia
il grido disperato degli umani.

O sei nel vero, vestale. — *E questo,*
questo tailleur mi dona?
— consunta dai sacrifici,
levigata dalle stagioni,
predata dai ceroni
sicut comoedians,
anchilosata dall'uso — *Ah, piccolo!*
stasera? —
Oh, quante zanzarucce,
petulanti ritornelli;
queste voci escluse!

Pour ne plus songer à tes sanglots,
bellezza viva e triste,
fiore di carta.

IV

Andante appassionato with brass and strings.
—*But I, I . . .* , cantabile wind of the street!
—*the brimming breasts, the lap, and you know . . .*
and even in Lethe you can't leave behind
the unbelievable savor of the flesh,
the snapping sails of my kisses,
the kisses . . .
and veins. They sing. —*But I, I!*
A bird that mocks
the desperate cry of humans.

O you're a vestal, in reality. —*And this,*
this suit, does it become me?
consumed by sacrifices,
polished by the seasons,
pillaged by the greasepaint
sicut comoedians,
paralyzed by use —*Ah, little one!*
this evening?
Oh, how many little gnats,
irritating refrains;
these excluded voices!

Pour ne plus songer à tes sanglots,
beauty alive and sad,
paper flower.

E non vivrai . . .

a Silvietta Contini

E se non credi nei tuoi figli e nei figli di questi,
forse, sei nato per morire.
E se ti senti offeso
quando la nipotina fa la pipì nel letto
e non t'inteneriscono gli occhioni
spauriti — e scivola
giù, e corre a rifugiarsi tra le gambe della nonna
e ti guarda con gli occhioni immensi
e attende un sorriso per sorriderti
o un'ombra nello sguardo
per scoppiare in pianto — tu
non sei degno di vivere
e non vivrai come me o come i fiumi,
immensi.

And You Won't Live . . .

to Silvietta Contini

And if you don't believe in your children and in their children
maybe you were born to die.
And if it offends you
when your little granddaughter pees in the bed
and if it doesn't touch your heart to see
her scared eyes—and she slides
down, and she runs for refuge between grandmother's legs
and she looks at you with great big eyes
and waits for a smile so she can smile at you
or a shadow in your look
to burst into tears—then you
aren't fit to live
and you won't live like me or like the rivers,
immense.

Il canto della speranza

per Alfredo Giop de Palchi, poeta

Les héros de demain sont les emprisonnés d'aujourd'hui
J.M. Domenach

Giorno per giorno
ora per ora
in vergine terra trasformiamo
aperta alle semente
presaga dell'alba abbrividita dai campani
l'arida ragnatela di questi giorni reclusi.

Il sangue
— non era ancor mietuto l'altro autunno
— fluisce caldo e silenzioso, segreta primavera,
sotto i nostri pensieri rivestiti
d'indifferenza. Attendiamo il domani.
Attendiamo che i giorni arino il campo,
senza fretta, e la linfa,
divorato il pensiero del passato,
in gemme verdi esploda
di là dalla corteccia. Esploda!

Siamo anime, un'anima sola.
Chi potrà ricondurre nel cielo scialbo
al limite delle mura
la nostra voce
resa divina dal pianto? È la nostra certezza,
chiara come il mattino
matura come l'estate.

The Song of Hope

for Alfredo Giop de Palchi, poet

Les héros de demain sont les emprisonnés d'aujourd'hui
J. M. Domenach

Day by day
hour by hour
in virgin land we transform—
open to seed
foretold by cowbells in the shivering dawn—
the barren cobweb of these imprisoned days.

The blood
—it hadn't yet been harvested last autumn—
is flowing hot and silent, a secret springtime,
under our thoughts covered over with
indifference. We're waiting for tomorrow.
We're waiting till the days unhurriedly
plow the field, and the sap,
having devoured the thought of the past,
let it explode beyond the shell
into green buds. Let it explode!

We are souls, one single soul.
Who can carry our voice
made divine by weeping
back through the colorless air
to the edge of the walls? It is our surety,
clear as the morning,
ripe as the summer.

Noi siamo
come il destino
ch'è più forte di noi;
come un chiaro mattino
c'impadroniamo del giorno
ed oltre, andiamo, il lamento di Pier delle Vigne,
sul Cranio Crucifero,
a prenderci per mano . . .
sul tetto degli scribi e dei profeti falsi,
con il Signore illuso
a prenderci per mano:

Oggi siam morti
per vivere domani.

Noi prepariamo la Terra.
La Terra è dolce come il grembo
materno. PREPARIAMO,
perché l'ari il tempo,
la nostra Terra.

We are
like destiny
that is stronger than we are;
like a clear morning
we take possession of the day
and beyond, we go on, the lament of Pier delle Vigne,
the Crossbearer on the Skull,
to join hands . . .
on the roof of the scribes and the false prophets,
with the deceived Lord,
to join hands:

Today we are dead
to live tomorrow.

We prepare the Earth.
The Earth is as sweet as a mother's
womb. LET US PREPARE,
so that time may plow there,
our Earth.

Sardegna

Altra pena non ho che di trovarmi
straniero ad ogni terra. Essere
il biondo turista che conosce
ogni scalo di mondo e, in ogni porto,
consuma nell'abbraccio un fantasma
e di sè cerca radici
morendo ogni giorno.

Mi dissero di querci immobili,
di mare sonnolento:
un'isola prosciugata dagli anni.
Mi dissero d'un'isola . . . — Signore,
ch'io non sia disperso!
— alla sua proda io tornerò
come un messaggio
sballottato dalle correnti.

Crescerà il mio sonno
sotto le arse mura dei nuraghi.

Sardinia

My sole affliction is to find myself
a stranger in every land. To be
the fairhaired tourist who knows the world's
every stopover and, in every port,
wears away a ghost in his embrace
and searches for his roots
dying every day.

They told me about the immobile oaks,
about the somnolent sea:
an island that's been dried up by the years.
They told me about an island . . . —Lord,
let me not be lost—!
I'll come back to its shore
like a message
bobbed and bandied by the currents.

My sleep will be deep
under the sunbaked walls of the nuraghes.

L'alleluja

Quando la mano adunca del giorno
s'allontana, delusa, dagli angeli: i selciati
falciano il cielo e il cuore,
con ululati di lupo.

Lavate il mio corpo, o gente,
con dolcezza fraterna! E voi,
sorelle silenziose,
dalle colline della Bibbia
portate doni di nardo, di letizia e di mirra.
Nardo odoroso e mirra
ed acqua limpida di fonte.
No, non il gallo
che fece vivere gli illusi!

Lavate,
lavate con dolcezza il corpo
che transita per nascere!
Lo spolverio delle strade togliete dalla pelle
e la paura verminosa del giorno
e la bruma delle effimere partenze.
Le fossili foreste delle case,
ove s'impaludava il cuore
nella distrutta architettura della carne
tra le rauche risa delle arpie
appollaiate sui bianchi canini dei cembali
e sugli archetti dei violini

The Alleluia

When the hooked hand of the day departs,
disappointed, from the angels: cobblestones
mow down the heavens and the heart,
howling like a wolf.

Wash my body, O people,
with fraternal gentleness! And you,
silent sisters,
from the hills of the Bible
bring gifts of spikenard, and of joy and myrrh.
Fragrant spikenard and myrrh
and clear water from the fountain.
No, not the rooster
who made the deluded live!

Wash,
gently wash the body
in transit to be born!
Remove the dust cloud of the roads from the skin
and the verminous fear of the day
and the haze of ephemeral departures.
The fossilized forests of the houses,
where the heart has become a swamp
in the ruined architecture of the flesh
amid the raspy laughter of the Harpies
perched on the white eyeteeth of harpsichords
and on the bows of violins

dai capelli lunghi e neri,
già dispaion oltre l'ultimo fanale . . .

Se rido tenero e triste è la coscienza
d'aver pagato il dono della vita,
da signore, con sangue.
Tutto ciò che mi tocca è scontato.

E una qualche pietà
abbiate del mio corpo:

le primavere, che in esso germogliavano
sonate dai sereni voli di colombe
ed assoluti occhi di albe
fugate dall'empito cieco del fiume,
tacciono. E i corvi,
gracchianti sulle torte braccia
dei pensieri, tacciono. Le acque
sposano i silenzi: un marmo
levigato dalle piogge e dai venti,
un faro spento
sullo sperone notturno.
Tanto ha palpitato questo vessillo umano!

Ora, dalle colline di Galaad
discendono le greggi
lattescenti nel fumo della sera.
Ora,
sui monti di Sion
i sacerdoti ripongono le spade e David,
nel tremito arioso delle lontananze,
spande sull'acque morte del lago
l'ultimo accordo . . .

made from long black hairs,
are already separating past the last lamp . . .

If I laugh softly and sadly it is in
awareness of having paid for the gift of life,
like a Lord, with blood.
All that touches me has been discounted.

And have some pity
on my body:

the springtimes, that have sprouted up in it
marked off by the peaceful flights of doves
and absolute eyes of dawns
put to flight by the river's blind impetus,
are silent. And the ravens,
cawing on the twisted limbs
of thoughts, are silent. The waters
wed the silences: a marble structure
polished by the rains and by the winds,
an extinguished lighthouse
on the nocturnal spur.
How much this human flag has waved and fluttered!

Now, from the hills of Gilead
the flocks descend
lactescent in the evening smoke.
Now,
on the mountains of Zion
the priests are putting their swords away and David,
in the airy tremor of distances,
spreads on the dead waters of the lake
the last accord . . .

Oh gente,
lavate il corpo
pronto agli amori del Signore,
e unguenti apparecchiate e nardo
ed alleluja
ALLELUJA!

Oh people,
wash the body
ready for the loves of the Lord,
and provide unguents and spikenard
and alleluia
ALLELUIA!

POESIE INEDITE
(1954–1960)

UNCOLLECTED POEMS
(1954–1960)

Bianco stupore è la tua fronte in quest'alba

Bianco stupore è la tua fronte in quest'alba.
Le stelle del tuo ebbro torpore
t'hanno abbandonato e neppure sorridi
tanto ti turbi del giorno.
È voce straniera la nuova diana
e ancora con tue gracili mani
t'inerbi — tua tristezza — all'ultime isole
della notte;
                              tuo pianto
dispera le forze. Macerie sono
le stagioni del tuo vivere. Un giorno,
un giorno solo ti prende valanga e ti spinge
inesorabile —
mente tra luci — allucinati desiri
impudica materia dei tuoi sogni celati —
verso l'altra sera.

Your Face Is a Blank Amazement in This Dawn

Your face is a blank amazement in this dawn.
The stars of your drunken numbness
have abandoned you and you don't even smile
you worry so about the day.
The new reveille is a foreign voice
and once again with your slender hands
you seed yourself—your sadness—to the last islands
of the night;
                    your tears
throw your strength into despair. Ruins
are the seasons of your living. One day,
one day an avalanche seizes you and pushes you
relentlessly—
mind amid lights—hallucinated desires
the lewd substance of your hidden dreams—
toward another evening.

O Babylon

O Babylon, le greggi
han pasturato tutta l'erba
solo uno stelo di rivolta
giace
al nostro davanzale.

Nel rombo degli aerei s'è spento
l'alto nitrito del cavallo
fratello
alla nostra infanzia.
E nel ricordo
è svanita l'Isola
e il sangue, forte,
della mia razza.

Supina-
mente ho sofferto e soffro
i tuoi mercati, o Babylon,
e vanità e sogno son caduti
cariatide abbracciata alla sera.

O Babylon

O Babylon, the flocks
have grazed all the grass
only one stalk of rebellion
lies
at our windowsill.

The roar of airplanes has drowned out
the high whinny of the horse
brother
of our childhood.
                                        And the Island
has vanished into memory
along with the strong blood
of my race.

                         Supine-
ly have I suffered and I suffer
your marketplaces, O Babylon,
and vanity and dream have fallen away
caryatid embraced at eventide.

Cavalluccio della speranza

Un cavalluccio impagliettato
si difende come può dai tafàni
nella piazzetta assolata.

Lo zoccolo batte
sul selciato
le ore fortunose dell'infanzia.

Quanto lontano mi sei
cavalluccio della speranza!

Little Horse of Hope

A little horse covered with netting
defends himself as best he can against
the horseflies in the sunny little square.

His hoof is beating
the eventful
hours of childhood on the cobblestone.

How far from me you are
little horse of hope!

Trasloco

Vento e cenere. Le querce
salutano il ricordo che trasloca.
Il Corso è un corso e il 25
solo un numero, un posto
nei rifiuti.

Cadono con le ghiande i coltelli
confitti nel cuore;
i sogni disperde e le nubi il vento
che uniforma l'altalena della vita:
polvere che acceca come l'odio,
l'amore se lo porta il carro
dello spazzino.
Cambiamo casa, insomma.

Mutare ringiovanisce,
sussurrare i vicini
alzando il bavero dell'indifferenza.
                                        Già,
coi capelli bianchi,
stordito in questo tempo senza tempo.
La luce svanisce all'angolo
e il bagaglio che mi trascino, pesante.

Moving

Wind and ashes. The oaks say
a farewell to the memory that is moving.
The Avenue is an avenue and the 25
only a number, a place
in the trash.

Knives fall with the acorns and are driven
into the heart;
dreams and clouds are scattered by the wind
that levels all the up and down of life:
dust that blinds like hatred,
love itself is carried off
by the streetsweeper's cart.
In short, we're changing houses.

Change rejuvenates,
the neighbors whisper
turning up the collar of indifference.
Already,
with white hair,
bewildered in this time outside of time.
The light is fading at the corner
and the baggage that I'm dragging, heavy.

da SCHEGGE D'ANIMA (1962)

from SPLINTERS OF SOUL (1962)

Delle avventure (1938–1945)

Adventures (1938–1945)

La baia incerta

La mia docile vela è giunta ormai
alla gelida riva, piano.
In penombra disincantai la vela
dai baci della brezza,
tra i murmuri dell'invisibile baia.

Un ippocampo s'ìnalbera e danza
— ma dove? le mani non hanno
l'arcana ansia del tempo —
mi sorride, tra rive di viola, attutito.

Ora so che la mia fuga
è sfiorita;
                                        un'ora m'avanza, forse
di più, a ritrovarmi. Baia che si fa certa.

The Uncertain Bay

My obedient sail has now arrived,
softly, at the icy shore.
In the shadow I disenchanted the sail
from the breeze's kisses,
amid the murmurs of the invisible bay.

There's a seahorse rearing up and dancing
—but where? my hands don't have
the arcane anxiety of time—
he smiles at me, muffled amid the violet banks.

Now I know that my escape
has withered;
                                        there's an hour left, maybe
more, to find myself. Bay that grows certain.

Afa

È infinito il roco canto — pigolìo dei piccoli —
nell'aia
e un cane che nessuno conosce
ansima tra grassa
e bluastra polverella di letamaio.

Inultilmente riguardo montagne accidiose
nell'afa, ho sete e caldo e canto
tristo nei sangui alla noia. Bassa
romba nell'aria una crociera di mosconi.

Heat

The tiny cheepers' hoarse song doesn't let up
on the threshing floor
                                        and a dog nobody knows
is panting in the greasy
and bluish powdery dust of the pigpen.

I aimlessly inspect the lazy mountains
in the heat, I'm hot and and thirsty and I have
a sad song of tedium in my veins. Low,
a flight of blowflies rumbles in the air.

Barche con musiche

Adolescente navigavo in bonaccia
per estivi balli: mazurchine fiorite
nell'ombra dei pàmpini.
                                        Baciavo
e, ribaciato, oh le ragazze, sospiravo
inquieto se a pelo di onda
filava lieve la luna.
                                Tanto mista
fortuna! e non sapevo, allora,
dolore salirmi cauto
al mio cuore. E a tenermi la mano
era il sereno. Da folle
io mi creava un mito,
e ragazzette baciavo e, ribaciato,
trasognato trasalivo e al bel tempo.

Quando silenziosa nel cielo
veleggiava la luna.

Boats with Music

As a teenager I cruised in a calm sea
through summer dances: little mazurkas
blooming in the shadow of vine leaves.
                                                  I kissed
the girls and, oh, kissed back, I gave
a restless sigh whenever the moon played lightly
on the surface of a wave.
                                    How mixed a fate
it was! and I didn't know, back then,
sorrow was growing cautiously
within my heart. It was a clear sky that
took my hand. In my madness
I made myself a myth,
and kissed the young girls and, kissed back, I started
up in a dreamy daze and in good weather.

When silently in the sky
the moon was sailing.

Ancora di barche e musiche

Non so umiliarmi per queste
torbide sere in cui barche
colme di corpi risalgono
come nel tuo regno infero, o Dante,
la corrente tortuosa, faticosamente
del mio sangue.
                                        Io solo so
vanità di queste effimere sabbie.
Stridono a sera tra i denti,
o nostra morte corporale, prima
che a precipizio nel giusto
cada il tuo tempo, mia integra morte.

More Boats and Music

I don't know how to humble myself
for these murky evenings when boats
filled with bodies resurface
as in your lower realm, O Dante,
in the laboriously winding current
of my blood.
                        I alone know
the emptiness of these ephemeral sands.
They grate at night in the teeth,
or our bodily death, before
when rightly and precipitately
your time falls, my entire death.

1946–1959

1946–1959

Le mosche

Le mosche intrecciavano un incubo
quando, nella luce verde del sogno,
apparve e disparve una ninfa
dalle mammelle gonfie di vita.

The Flies

The flies wove a nightmare when,
in the green light of the dream,
there appeared and disappeared
a nymph with the swollen breasts of life.

Solo un dirupo

Solo un dirupo mi rimane pensile sul mare
calcinato dal sole
e qualche ago amaro
di pino:
                destarsi
nel primo mattino
e attendere
l'onda che m'infranga.

All I Have Left

All I have left is a cliff hanging over the sea
limed by the sun
and some bitter needles
of pine:
            waking up
in the early morning
and waiting for
the wave that will break me.

Caffè

Nel giorno che si sfalda
gli angeli siedono battuti,
ai tavoli di ferro. Pàlpebra
pesante, angeli battuti.

A colpi morbidi l'azzardo
tentano, barando, (gli occhi
fuggono la folla: assopire
l'agonia ignota di quei passi!)
l'innocenza.
                        I ragni
brucano, discreti,
i morti fogli dei giornali.

Nell'improvvisa luce vanno
e vengono i profeti, bianchi
uccelli di palude (gli angeli
gli occhi sollevano, deserti . . .),
camerieri dall'aspetto stanco.

Cafè

In the disintegrating day
angels are sitting, beaten,
at iron tables. Heavy
eyelids, beaten angels.

They gamble with soft
shots, cheating (their eyes
avoid the crowd: to soothe
the unknown pain of those moves!),
innocence.
                    Spiders
delicately nibble
the dead leaves of newspapers.

In the sudden light prophets
go and come, white
wading birds (the angels
raise their eyes, forlorn . . .),
tired-looking waiters.

Silenzio

Pensavo al silenzio e lo vedevo, lieve,
respirare nelle foglie,
nei sistri delle cicale: Un fumo,
sul tetto,
nel quale tremolava la memoria.

Sospinto e risospinto dall'afa
toccai la curva dolce
del cielo.

La luna è ferma sulle labbra.

Silence

I thought of silence and I saw it, light,
breathing in the leaves,
in the sistrums of cicadas: a wisp of smoke,
on the roof,
and memory was flickering in it.

Driven further and further by the heat
I touched the gentle curve
of the sky.

The moon is motionless on my lips.

Non conoscerò

Non conoscerò i tonfi sordi del cane
nel padule, spenti da uno scroscio
d'acque; e subito odore di terra.
Né conoscerò l'occhio intelligente
della serpe: un arabesco di sogni
congelati. Sàlpano gli aironi
alle foreste azzurre.

I Won't Know

I won't know the dull thudding of the dog
in the marshes, smothered by a roar
of water; and suddenly a scent of earth.
And neither will I know the acute eye
of the serpent: an arabesque of frozen
dreams. The herons are setting out
for the blue forest.

Ancora delle avventure

Further Adventures

Città piovosa e semaforo

Il tempo puoi sentirlo nel *rosso*.
Fermiamoci un attimo in ascolto:
il disperato coltello dei pompieri
strazia la pioggia, s'apre un viale
di attonite querci
da un capo all'altro del cuore.

Verde — :
Ora puoi dare un tocco
di avventuroso carminio al tuo sorriso;
puoi sciogliere il groppo di lagrime
e andare, smemorando, tremula seppia
che ha dato già tutto l'inchiostro.
Due libbre di speranza
avvolte nelle
ULTIMISSIME NOTIZIE
della sera. *Giallo*. Indifferenza
agli occhi delle case: « Una ragazza
dall'apparente età di 30 delusioni
e problemi tentati,
uncinata dai morsi delle strade,
ha rinunciato ai suoi giorni
di attesa . . . »
A goccia a goccia si sfanno
nelle pozzanghere della coscienza
le nostre realtà.

Rainy City and Traffic Light

You can hear time in the *red*.
Let's stop for a moment to listen:
the desperate knife of the firemen
rends the rain, opens an avenue
of astonished oaks
from one end of the heart to the other.

Green—:
Now you can put a dab
of audacious carmine in your smile;
you can melt the lump of your tears
and go off in a fog, a squirming cuttlefish
that has already squirted all its ink.
Two pounds of hope
wrapped in the
LATEST NEWS
of the evening. *Yellow*. Indifference
to the eyes of the houses: "A girl
of the apparent age of 30 attempted
problems and disappointments,
hooked by the morsels of the streets,
has given up her days
of waiting . . ."
Drop by drop our realities
dissolve into puddles of
consciousness.

Come un pallone frenato

Un intero giorno di sole ho goduto
amato dalle gracili strade.
Tante mani di sicomoro
tardive e inquiete
indugiavano sui selciati del sangue.

Io guardavo le rossigne bocche
a cuore
delle donne. Una mano di vento
dava senso alle cose.
Come un pallone frenato
oscillavo.

Like a Captive Balloon

I enjoyed a whole day of sunshine
loved by the slender streets.
How many late and restless
hands of sycamores
dawdled on the cobblestones of blood.

I looked at the reddish heart-shaped
mouths
of women. A touch of wind
gave sense to things.
Like a captive balloon
I swayed.

Blues dell'attesa

Solo il vino può consolarmi nell'attesa, amore.
Solo il vino può consolarmi.

Io sono come morta quando le tue mani
la tua bocca
vanno lontane dal mio sangue.
Non sono più una donna se tu non mi baci
ma uno squallido orto vangato dal tifone.

Affretta il tuo passo, amore, prima che l'alba
schiarisca
e mi costringa a chiudere le imposte.
Oh quanto lunga è la notte ed io son sola
tra il grido dei corvi e l'ansietà del mio cuore!
Oh, solo il vino può consolarmi nell'attesa,
amore!

Solo il vino può consolarmi.

Waiting Blues

Only wine can console me while I'm waiting, love.
Only wine can console me.

I'm just like a dead thing when your hands
your mouth
are gone far away from my blood.
I'm no woman anymore if you don't kiss me
but a dreary garden spaded by a typhoon.

Pick up your pace, my love, before the dawn
lightens
and makes me pull the shutters closed.
Oh the night's so long and I'm alone
with the cry of crows and my heart's anxiety!
Oh, only wine can console me while I'm waiting,
love.

Only wine can console me.

A mia moglie

Il male ch'era in me
come nebbia sospesa
ho bruciato
nell'anfora casta
della tua giovinezza. Rimorso
che mi trascino
immemore.

                In questa
attonita alba, nonostante
le scorie doloranti, dal crogiuolo
svettano, tremula aurora,
soccorrendo la speranza,
le nostre bimbe.

To My Wife

The sickness that was in me
like a hanging fog
I have burned off
in the pure amphora
of your youth. Remorse
that I drag along
oblivious.

                    In this
astonished dawn, in spite of
the painful slag, from the crucible
they rise, tremulous sunrise,
to rescue hope,
our girls.

Il ricordo

Il meriggio s'apriva come un mare
di tedio,
immoto.
Eppure fuggivamo a un porto
d'incoscienza, inutilmente.

Il ricordo è una diga
che duole.

Recollection

The noontide opened like a sea
of tedium,
motionless.
And yet we fled to a port
of unconsciousness, in vain.

Recollection is a dam
that aches.

Pioggia

Un po' di sole, Signore!

Dopo le piogge autunnali
dell'inverno
e della primavera
ancor piove, a diluvio, Signore!
Piove, beninteso, su tutta la gamma
dei nostri peccati
(anche sulle nostre speranze, però
— le speranze riposte sui figli,
sulla loro innocenza).

Su tutta la terra, amica e nemica, le erbe
hanno radici disfatte.
E muore, Signore,
la verde erba,
verde come le nostre speranze
(e, con esse, l'humus
che la pioggia disperde
scoprendo la roccia
nera
dei nostri peccati).

Un po' di sole, Signore!

Rain

A bit of sunshine, Lord!

After the rains of autumn
of winter
and spring
it's still raining, in a deluge, Lord!
It's raining, naturally, on the whole range
of our sins
(also, however, on our hopes
—the hopes placed on our children,
on their innocence).

On the whole earth, friend and foe, the roots
of the grass have been destroyed.
                                                It's dying, Lord,
the green grass,
green like our hopes
(and, with them, the humus
scattered by the rain
laying bare the black
rock
of our sins).

Lord, a bit of sunshine!

Donna e primavera

I

Il cielo dilunga le sue braccia.
È dolce camminare in questa indifferenza
luminosa.
Dove nacqui non so
per certo non mi disfece Maremma.
Parliamo d'altro per favore.

A ciascun che mi guarda
io dico: Amore, il volto
me l'han rapito le lacrime.
E a ciascun che mi chiede
io dico: Il mio passato
se l'è inghiottito
un soldato delle Ardenne.

E se insiste: Fu a un ballo mascherato.
Lui disse che gli piacevo così
le carni frollate dalla guerra
l'anima distrutta dalla guerra.

Disse ch'io ero una donnina *chic*.
Mi condusse
dove il sobborgo si fa verde
e il verde si sciolse nel palpito degli occhi . . .

Poi rise
e il riso sonava come un mare disperato.

Woman and Springtime

I

The sky is stretching out its arms.
It's pleasant to be walking in this radiant
indifference.
I don't know where I was born
but I'm certain Maremma didn't undo me.
Let's talk about something else if you don't mind.

To everyone who looks at me
I say: Love, its tears
have ravished my face.
And to everyone who asks me
I say: My past
has been swallowed up
by a soldier of the Ardennes.

And if they insist: It was at a masked ball.
He said that he liked me so
flesh softened by the war
soul destroyed by the war.

He said I was a very *chic* young woman.
He led me
where the suburb is green
and the green melted in the fluttering of my eyes . . .

Then he laughed
and his laugh sounded like a despondent sea.

II

E se insisti: Io sono qui e parlo
e parlo . . .
                    Tempo per amare,
tempo per ricordare.
                                Il mio passato
se lo è preso il soldato delle Ardenne.
Oh, io volevo morire, certo,
ma lui rideva e il riso
frusciava via come un mare disperato.
Ce n'est pas possible
pas possible . . . e un paio
di seriche calze m'ha donato
e una rosa rossa
di sangue
a mezzo il cuore.

Voi sapete poi
come han fine certe storie:
Si sfanno in coda a un treno lontanante
con l'ultima speranza
con l'ultimo dolore lancinante.
Sempre e sempre le solite storie.

Rientrando mi soffermai sulla piazza
con gli occhi spenti
una domenica d'aprile.
Il concerto mi rese come pazza
pazza e il sangue,
ondoso sul ritmo del valzer,
mi rapiva mi rapiva
sventolando le mie carni al sole.

II

And if you insist: I'm here and I'm talking
and talking . . .
                    Time for loving,
time for remembering.
                              My past
was taken by the soldier of the Ardennes.
Oh, I wanted to die, of course,
but he laughed and his laugh
rustled away like a despondent sea.
Ce n'est pas possible
pas possible . . . and he gave me
a pair of silk stockings
and a blood-red
rose
through the heart.

You know after all
how certain stories finish:
At the end they dissolve to a train moving away
with the last hope
with the last stabbing pain.
Forever and forever the same old stories.

Coming back I lingered on the square
with deadened eyes
one April Sunday.
The concert made me like a crazy woman
crazy and my blood,
billowing on the rhythm of the waltz,
ravished me ravished me
fluttering my flesh in the sunlight.

E ho dimenticato.
Da quella lontana domenica d'aprile
io tesso e ritesso la mia vita
ogni giorno.

Ed ora parliamo d'altro, per favore.

And I forgot.
Out of that April Sunday so far away
I compose and recompose my life
every day.

Now let's talk about something else, if you don't mind.

Casa di Liguria

Nella sera che plana alla tua casa
dolce, d'autunno: I rimorsi, come foglie
divelte, bussano alla porta.

I figli hanno solo rimorsi: Sospirano,
lievi, sull'uscio fermo di casa.

I tuo corpo, piegato dal vento acròno
dei rimorsi (tu,
anima astata e solare),
s'aggruma
al rifluire lento dei ricordi:
Tu ne parli con Dio, le mani
congiunte sulle poste
del rosario . . .
È di ieri soltanto il nostro grido
felice
di rondine: Partire, partire!

E son rimasti i rimorsi, come foglie
divelte
nella sera che plana alla tua casa.

House in Liguria

In the evening that comes gliding to your sweet
house, in autumn: regrets, like stripped-away
leaves, tap at the door.

The children have nothing but regrets: They sigh,
lightly, on the closed entrance of the house.

Your body, bent by the seasonless wind
of regrets (you,
spear-shaped and solar spirit),
grows clotted
in the slow ebb of regrets:
You talk about it to God, your hands
joined on the beads
of the rosary . . .
Our joyous swallowlike cry: Fly away!
fly away!
belongs only to yesterday.

And the regrets remain, like stripped-away
leaves
in the evening that comes gliding to your house.

Innocenza

Albero
albero bello
sei antico e fresco
sei l'albero bello dell'infanzia.

I tuoi verdi capelli
hanno nidi di gioia
che a notte esplodono
impazziti come violini
fermi sul querulo
balbettìo del ruscello.

Sei mio padre e mia madre
il fratello
che dona una mano
una casa
alla memoria
il dito che spiana
la ruga del tempo.

Da quel giramondo ch'io sono
volubile a tutti gli amori
solo in te mi ritrovo
alla tua ombra distendo
la voce discorde
della Città.

Albero
albero bello
innocenza.

Innocence

Tree
beautiful tree
you are ancient and fresh
you are the beautiful tree of childhood.

Your green hair
has nests of joy
that explode madly
at night like violins
fixed on the eloquent
babble of the brook.

You are my father and my mother
the brother
who lends a hand
a home
to memory
the finger that smooths
the wrinkle of time.

From the vagrant that I am
fickle in every love
only in you I recover myself
in your shadow I soften
the clanging voice
of the city.

Tree
beautiful tree
innocence.

Le madri giungeranno

Udirlo il grido dilatarsi
snodando la sua lunga coda
alla radice dei castani
poi spegnersi umano
sulla corrente del fiume.

È la vita di noi esclusi
assiepati in questa foresta
d'inganni
di fuggitive illusioni.

È il nostro sangue commisto
che grida
dagli ultimi spalti
il dolore dell'esilio.

Le madri giungeranno
con la luce del cuore
tra i castani braccati
a ricomporre gli straziati tramonti
della nostra innocenza.

E sterpi e sterpi coglieranno
per un falò
che illumini il viaggio nel buio.

The Mothers Will Come

To hear the cry expand
extending its long tail
at the root of the chestnut tree
and then vanish human
on the current of the river.

It's our life the excluded
hedged round in this forest
by deceptions
by fugitive illusions.

It's our mixed blood
that cries out
the pain of exile from
the last battlements.

The mothers will come
with the light of the heart
amid the hunted chestnut trees
to recompose the lacerated sunsets
of our innocence.

And they will gather twigs and branches
for a bonfire
to illuminate the journey into the dark.

da VIAGGIO NEL BUIO (1969)

from JOURNEY INTO THE DARK (1969)

Il vento gonfiava i panni stesi
nel dormitorio. Andava la memoria
a ritroso verso agavi
e limoni di Liguria
                              incontro
a un ragazzo che sognava velieri
pescando arselle
sui frangiflutti.

Il veliero ha circumnavigato i desideri
e ha gettato l'àncora
contro il verdezolfo del Miseno.
Le vele pendono trafitte.
Solo i pochi panni stesi
da una parete a l'altra
gonfia il vento.

Procida 1947

The wind was swelling the laundry hanging up
in the dormitory room. Memory ran
backward toward the agaves
and lemons of Liguria
                              a rendezvous
with a boy who dreamed of windjammers
fishing for mussels
on the breakwater.

The windjammer's circumnavigated his desires
and dropped anchor
in the green sulphur of Miseno.
The sails are drooping, struck.
The wind is swelling only
the laundry hanging from one wall
to the other.

Procida, 1947

Sul fondale giallo di pozzolana
di una silenziosa domenica
pomeriggio
                    quando
si è già detto tutto e i treni
hanno sferragliato nella piana
brulla
portandoci lontano.

E s'è già detto tutto anche il non detto
di noi
delle nostre malattie
e si è come uomini di paglia
incendiati dalle vene
spenti marinai ch'ànno speso
fin l'ultimo spicciolo di paga
alla taverna dei ricordi.

Allora può zampillare nel silenzio
spericolato aquilone
il grido d'un fanciullo
di là dal muro di cinta:

l'ascoltiamo dementi
e tremuli con gli occhi
naufragati nell'azzurro.

Civitavecchia 1950

On the yellow backdrop of pozzolana
on a quiet Sunday
afternoon
                    when
everything was already said and the trains
were clattering across the barren
plain
taking us far away.

And all was already said even what we left unsaid
of us
of our maladies
and we are like men of straw
ignited by their veins
spent sailors who have spent
the last penny of their pay
at the tavern of memories.

So then a reckless kite
the cry of a boy on the other
side of the surrounding wall
can spring up in the silence:

we listen to it demented
and tremulous with our eyes
foundering in the blue.

Civitavecchia, 1950

Le betulle tremavano sull'argine del fiume
e calabroni impazzivano
nel torrido vento.
                                        Ed era
penoso, credimi baciarti
sentendomi sconvolto dai tuoi occhi
assiri e verdi come un'erba
su cui dolce scivoli la luce.
Un'ansia di predarti e il cuore
di non violare, acrobata da circo,
il tuo mattino bianco
mi tenevano sospeso sul filo.

Ma tu volevi offrire come un ponte
la tua segreta esistenza al mio
solitario vagare — stanco
ed inquieto di peccati ignoti
che dolevano, rimorso
— per confortarmi e fare
di due mondi un nido.

Millesimo 1954

The birches trembled on the bank of the river
and hornets went mad
in the scorching wind.
                                        And it was
painful, believe me, to kiss you
feeling disconcerted by your eyes
that were Assyrian and green as grass
over which the light glides tenderly.
A fear of preying on you and the heart
not to violate, circus acrobat,
your white morning,
they kept me there suspended on the wire.

But you desired to extend your secret
existence like a bridge to my
solitary wandering—fatigued
and uneasy over unknown sins
that pained me, and regret
—to comfort me and make
out of two worlds one nest.

Millesimo, 1954

Messa vespertina

I

I conformisti gli ipocriti L'uccisero
sulla soglia del Cranio
poi bighellonarono chiacchierando
sbirciando il dondolio degli estinti
al ponentino
                    una sera
che il venticello affebbriva sui monti di Sion
con mano inquieta
                              indugiando perplessi a udire
fra dense nubi d'incenso
l'anacronistico canto gregoriano.

L'empie donne conseguenti e leziose
ripudiavano lo Spirito e i figli
ripudiavano il Padre
cinguettando passeggiando ridendo:
— Ci ha lasciati. Finalmente
possiamo disperare.
                              Il sole
si nascose dietro le cimose delle case.

Evening Mass

I

The conformists the hypocrites they put Him to death
on the threshold of the Skull
then loitering about and chattering
sneaking a glance at the swaying of the deceased
in the westerly breeze
                                        one evening
when a light wind fevered over the mountains of Zion
with a troubled hand
                                        lingering in perplexity to listen
amid dense clouds of incense
to the anachronistic Gregorian chant.

The blasphemous women following and simpering
repudiated the Spirit and the children
repudiated the Father
twittering and sauntering and laughing:
—He's gone away from us. Now finally
we can abandon hope.
                                        The sun
hid itself behind the selvages of the houses.

II

Gargotte caffeucci e bar al cromo
tendevano le braccia ai soldati
in libera uscita
mescevano assenzio agli innocenti
gioia alle marcolfe
coca-cola ai capelloni
                                        una sera
che sulla soglia del Cranio
— l'occhio di Barabba tremolò —
L'uccise la folla in Israele.

I camerieri
piroettando fra i tavoli
riscuotendo litigando ammonendo
effondono la buona novella
con gli ultimi spiccioli di Borsa
e i residui commenti sulla guerra fredda
(la morte è inseparabile). Incalzata
dai jukebox fiorisce
bandiera a mezz'asta
sullo stretto scalo delle case
l'ultima diàspora.
                                        Occhiali neri
sullo sguardo e vento e sale il coro
parole d'ambascia esala: *Senza fine*
Tu trascini la nostra vita
senza un attimo di respiro . . . Esala:
Senza fine.
Oh i claxon tinnuli sulla fuga
morbida *Alleluja*
Alleluja
dei pneumatici. È morto! Esulta

II

Chophouses and small cafés and chromed
coffeeshops opened up their arms to soldiers
out on leave
they poured absinthe for the innocents
joy for the clodhoppers
Coca-Cola for the hippies
                                        one evening
when on the threshold of the Skull
—Barabbas's eye was twitching—
the crowd put Him to death in Israel.

The waiters
pirouetting between the tables
collecting quarreling admonishing
pouring out the good news
along with the latest spare change from the Market
and leftover observations about the Cold War
(death is inseparable). Closely
pursued by the jukebox
the flag at half mast
over the cramped terminal of the houses
the last diaspora flourishes.
                                        Dark glasses
over the eyes and the wind and the chorus rises
exhaling words filled with distress: *Without end*
You drag us through our lives
without a moment of reprieve . . . Exhaling:
Without end.
Oh the horns jangling over the smooth
escape *Alleluia*
Alleluia
of tires. He is dead! The crowd

la folla e battono le mani a tempo
i giovani
a tempo su di un letto d'ottone
fiutando caninamente un exit
con stridor di denti ansando
leccando eiaculando la speranza.

Piroettando arraffando mance i camerieri
vociando inseguendo la speranza:
Senza fine, senza fine.

III

Non possiamo distrarci
né a Creta né a Pafo o Barabba.
Un piede nella vita un diesis.
Svagato gironzolo slittando
su sporche sillabe di cronaca
cogliendo a volo di rondine gli azzurri
e i rossi e i gialli al neon
di quella sera ermetica e svenata
carpendo i sospiri il canto i claxon
e il vuoto e il vento e le promesse
e i silenzi astiosi
le carezze indifferenti e i denti
che stridono sul letto
i tarocchi rovesciati sul tavolo
il cieco gregge degli illusi
degli ubbriachi di fede
                                        chiedendomi
che alba attendano mai quegli occhi spenti
quegli assassini che guatano

exults and claps its hands in time
the young
moving in time on a brass bed
sniffing out an exit like a dog
with the gnashing of the teeth
panting licking ejaculating hope.

Pirouetting grabbing up their tips
the waiters bellowing and chasing hope:
Without end, without end.

III

Nothing can distract us
either at Crete or at Paphos or Barabbas.
One foot in life a diesis.
I wander around diverted sliding over
the grubby syllables of the report
catching in the flight of swallows all
the neon blues and reds and yellows of
that hermetic and exsanguinated evening
teasing out the sighs the chant the horns
the emptiness the wind the promises
and the resentful silences
the indifferent caresses and the teeth
gnashing on the bed
the Tarot cards turned over on the table
the blind flock of the deluded
of those who are drunk on faith
                                        asking myself
what dawn those listless eyes ever expect
those murderers who stare

sulla soglia del Cranio
il frutto dell'azione.

Il sacrificio trascorse nell'aria vuota
nelle pigre coscienze
e all'*Ite*
missa est scoppiò l'applauso, un tuono.
Al venerdì letterario,
le rondini fecero il nido nell'occhio di Barabba,
il conferenziere concluse:
                                        In noi
è una baia
ove sirene lanciano rauchi appelli
nella nebbia
rauchi appelli (isolate) nella nebbia
invocando il Pilota che ci guidi
alla salvezza.

                              Nel molle incenso
che a folate . . . Ognuno
credesi in pace sui monti d'Israele.

Roma 1967

on the threshold of the Skull
at the fruit of their act.

The sacrifice passed by in the empty air
in the lazy consciences
and at *Ite*
missa est a thunder of applause exploded.
On literary Friday,
the swallows made their nest in Barabbas's eye,
the lecturer concluded:
                                        There is
a bay inside us
where sirens launch their hoarse appeals
in the fog
hoarse appeals (isolated) in the fog
calling out to the Pilot who guides us
to our salvation.

                              In the gentle incense
that in puffs . . . Everyone
believes himself in peace on the mountains of Israel.

Rome, 1967

POESIE INEDITE
(1960–1979)

UNCOLLECTED POEMS
(1960–1979)

Si fa sera

Ora che i passeri bisbigliano
quieti nel fondo del fogliame
io corro a te come fa il bimbo
al seno della madre.

It's Getting Dark

Now that the sparrows are murmuring
quietly in the depths of the foliage
I run to you the way a little boy
runs to his mother's breast.

Non vi è che la pazienza: attendere.
Non illuminarti di gioia
alla primalba,
né piangere al tramonto.
Non lamentarti
non porgere esca al riso.
Accogli in silenzio la tua giornata.
Fa come la linfa
che alla stagione giusta
esplode con le gemme.
Se il tempo ha il passo lento
corri
se è lesto siedi.
Addormenta i ricordi col vino rosso
e non ascoltare consigli.
Né carità.
Né crudeltà.
Segui come fa il fiume nel suo alveo
la strada dei tuoi giorni.
Non fare passi in più
non arretrarti a mezza via.
Non vi è che la pazienza: attendere.
Sei tu che decidi.

Patience is all there is for you, so wait.
Don't light yourself up with joy
at dawn,
or weep at sunset.
Don't complain
don't troll bait for laughter.
Accept your day in silence.
Be like the sap
that bursts into bud
in its proper season.
If time has a slow tread
run
if it's speedy sit.
Anesthetize your memories with red wine
and don't listen to advice.
Or charity.
Or cruelty.
Follow the highway of your days just as
the river does its bed.
Don't take too many steps
don't pull back in the middle of the way.
Patience is all there is for you, so wait.
It's your decision.

Presentazione

Moglie e figli ho presentato
a mio padre
tra le vigne rosse, in un ottobre
tiepido. Mio padre ci sorrise
accarezzandoci, col vento che fluiva,
dolce, dalle colline, i volti
e gli abiti di festa.

Questo da tempo ormai,
era il voto cui adempiere,
da quando ci lasciammo con gli addii;
ed era il mio rimorso.

Ma il tempo risana e mentre
ilare mia moglie componeva
sul marmo i crisantemi della pace
egli mi andava discorrendo,
coi passeri ciarlieri e i pettirossi,
ciò che da mesi io ripeteva ai figli,
ricordando: « Un pane
e tutti uniti ».

Intorno,
contro quel cielo svenato,
tra le vigne, i nipotini
intrecciavano ghirlande
d'allegrie.

Presentation

I presented my wife and children
to my father
amid the red vineyards, in a mild
October. My father smiled at us
caressing us, with the wind that streamed,
gently, from the hills, the faces
and the festive clothes.

For a long time now, there was
this vow to be fulfilled,
from when we left each other with farewells;
and it was my regret.

But time heals, and once
while my wife was cheerfully arranging
chrysanthemums of peace upon the marble
he began to say to me,
with the garrulous sparrows and the robins,
what I repeated to the children for months,
remembering: "A loaf of bread
and all of us together."

                                        All around,
against that washed-out sky, amid
the vineyards, the little grandchildren
were weaving garlands
of gaiety.

A un tratto sviai

A un tratto sviai per una strada di campagna,
primo: l'erba
falciata s'assiepava come
per un finale di giovinezza.

Il sole era enorme,
enorme la memoria. A mezza costa,
e per le bacche rosse dei pruni
il dono punse nel costato,
tolsi le scarpe e,
sbadigliando,
fornicai col nulla.

I Suddenly Went Astray

I suddenly went astray on a country road,
the first one there: the mowed
grass was all around me as if
in a farewell to youth.

The sun was immense,
immense the memory. Halfway up the hill,
and through the red berries of the thornbushes
the gift stung me in the side,
I took off my shoes and,
yawning,
I fornicated with nothing.

Quando t'incontrai, o Sileno,
sulle rive del Tirso
abbassasti lo sguardo:
sapevi quanta pena
m'avrebbe accompagnato
nella vita.

When I met up with you, O Silenus,
on the banks of the Tirso
you lowered your eyes:
you knew how much pain
would have come along with me
in my life.

Cielo vivo

Amo gli occhi giulivi
dei bambini, coli
di chiarità, ed i corpi
flessuosi di chi urge
sul ramo della vita
come l'adolescente;
ed i petti virili ove s'annida
l'impeto della specie;
e i tremuli fiori dei meli
vibranti nell'aria d'aprile
e questo cielo vuoto di nubi
così dilatato sul mondo —
che grida — lo sento — che grida
presenze divine.

Living Sky

I love the joyful eyes
of little children, sieves
of brightness, and the lithe
bodies of those who press
upon the branch of life
as adolescents do;
and manly breasts in which
the strength of the species nests;
and fluttering appletree flowers
vibrant in April air
and this unclouded sky
stretched wide over the world—
that shouts—I hear it—shouts
of divine presences.

Chi ci salverà?

È l'ora in cui, delusi, invochiamo
un mezzo che ci riporti a casa.
                                        Al crocevia
volteggiando angeli di nebbia
e il tram non giunge. Solo
qualche platano dà vita
alle prime ombre della sera.
Nel fondo, alla foschia, una luce
rossastra occhieggia e il cuore
ha trasalimenti nel vuoto dell'attesa.

Poi ti avvedi
a uno stridere di denti sulla curva
che non era il tram. Sgomenti
attendiamo il presagio: Chi
ci salverà?

Who Will Save Us?

It's the hour when, disheartened, we invoke
a means of getting home again.
At the intersection
angels of fog are circling
and the streetcar doesn't come. Only
a few plane trees give life
to the first shadows of the evening.
Off in the background, in the mist, there is
a reddish light emerging and the heart
quickens in the emptiness of waiting.

Then you notice
with a grinding of teeth that it wasn't
the streetcar around the bend. Dismayed
we wait for the omen: Who
will save us?

O voi, fanciulle che sul lido andate
— e il mare si prostra a vellicarvi i piedi
— ridendo e serie e spinte da una forza
ineluttabile: io vi guardo passare, me,
vecchio Tiresia, che so il destino cui andate
incontro, la ferocia dei giorni
che vi attende
e i sogni.

Chiaro di luna
salivi a grado a grado
sul Tirso
e andava già coi flutti
al mare

sotto il trepido e irridente
sguardo di Sileno

andavo
chiaro di luna
a grado a grado
con la mia pena
d'essere
e il Tirso
piangeva già la mia sorte
d'esiliato.

O you, young girls who go out on the beach
—and the sea prostrates itself to tickle your feet
—laughing and serious and urged by a force
that is ineluctable: I watch you pass, me,
old Tiresias, knowing the destiny
you're going to meet, the fierceness of the days
waiting for you
and the dreams.

Moonlight
grew gradually
on the Tirso
and went with the flow
to the sea

under the anxious and derisive
gaze of Silenus

moonlight went
gradually
with my
torment
of being
and the Tirso
mourned for my exile's
destiny.

Un giorno di novembre

I gigli sono appassiti.
Le cavalle pregne galoppano
nella brughiera nitrendo
all'incombere lampotuonante delle nubi.

Formeranno il Governo? chiedono
attorno sfogliando l'ultime
cronache della sera.
Lo formeranno?
I gigli appassiranno ancora.
Ancora le torbide cavalle
alte nitrendo galopperanno
nella squallida brughiera
incontro alle nubi basse.

Poi interverrà l'Onorevole saccente:
fiutando le acque dell'autunno
proporrà la crisi
come un caso di coscienza.

Laetificabat iuventutem meam
e potrò dire: *Introibo?* Tu
occhi verdi allungati fino
alle mura di Nabucodonosor,
tu molle adagiata sul divano
tenera alla fiamma
chiusa alla speranza
appassita coi gigli e viva

One Day in November

The lilies have withered.
The pregnant mares are galloping
over the moor whinnying
at the threatening thunder and lightning from the clouds.

Are they going to form a Government? they ask
around as they leaf through the latest
evening news.
                    Are they going to form one?
The lilies will wither further still.
Still the troubled mares
will gallop whinnying loudly
over the dismal moor
toward the low clouds.

Then the Honorable know-it-all will intervene:
sniffing the waters of autumn
he'll submit the crisis
as a matter of conscience.

Laetificabat iuventutem meam
and will I be able to say: *Introibo?* You,
green eyes stretched as far
as the walls of Nebuchadnezzar,
you settled softly on the sofa
tender to the flame
closed to hope
withered with the lilies and alive

contro la mia titubanza.
Tu, Eva, accetterai un sorso
dirai che sei stanca,
dirai: Ho vagato tutto il giorno
pei negozi del centro, in galleria,
in un cinema dalle mani attaccaticce,
a una tavola calda
respirando le caprine voci dei maschi.
Ora, qui, m'intenerisco ai gigli che si sfanno
e nel sangue ho come un nitrire di cavalle
selvatiche in cerca d'un rifugio
ove partorire in pace.

L'Onorevole saccente scuote il capo
volto il dorso al caminetto
pensa se non è il caso di sciogliere
il dilemma con un compromesso.
La causa, dice, ha i suoi diritti;
un uomo è un uomo . . .
Ahimé, quante realtà che appaiono già nostre
si stemperano poi nella palude
dell'indecisione!
Prendete questi gigli, ad esempio, o me,
soffocato dalle nubi basse,
implorante una luce che mi assista
per il lungo viaggio nel buio.

in opposition to my dithering.
You, Eve, will accept a sip
you'll say that you are tired,
you'll say: I have been wandering all day
through the shops downtown, in the gallery,
in a movie theater full of squishy hands,
at a cafeteria
inhaling the goatish voices of the males.
Now, here, I'm touched by the decomposing lilies
and in my blood I feel something like the whinnying
of wild mares that are searching for a safe place
where they can give birth in peace.

The Honorable know-it-all shakes his head
turned toward the back of the fireplace
he wonders if it's not a chance to resolve
the dilemma with a compromise.
The case, he says, has its rights;
a man is a man . . .
Alas, how many realities that already match ours
are melted away in the marsh
of indecision!
Take these lilies, for instance, or take me,
suffocated by the low-hanging clouds,
crying out for a light to help me find
my way through the long journey into the dark.

Ahimé, Signore, sono stanco di lottare contro l'ipocrisia
di combattere contro me stesso
stanco di questo levarsi del sole
di questo morire ogni sera
stanco di udire
di capire di dolermi e di ridere
di vivere e dormire
stanco della primavera dell'estate dell'autunno
e dell'inverno
dei germogli
e delle foglie che scivolano per terra.
Stanco dell'odio e dell'amore.
Come Leopold Bloom vorrei sedermi sul water
a leggere la cronaca cittadina
poi tirarmi su le brache
e andare.

Alas, Lord, I'm tired of fighting against hypocrisy
of struggling against myself
I'm tired of this rising of the sun
of this dying every evening
tired of hearing
of knowing of complaining and of laughing
of living and sleeping
tired of spring of summertime of autumn
and of winter
of the buds
and of the leaves that slide along the ground.
I'm tired of hatred and I'm tired of love.
I wish I could sit myself down on the toilet
like Leopold Bloom to read the news of the city
and then just pull my trousers up
and go.

Le mie bambine

Due betulle tremule
nel sole
amore chiama
all'alba
col grido fugace delle rondini.

Gli occhi già presi dalla vita
attendono l'evento
le mani fragili materne
cullano la bambola.

Da quali remote plaghe
siete giunte
irreali
a queste rive dolenti?
È un sole il vostro vivere
che abbaglia:
mi sento dilungare
come un fiume.

Nuovi tormenti mi prendono
ma dolci
ch'esplodono nel ridere
a volte mi stringono la gola
con un pianto fresco
che porta in Paradiso.

My Little Girls

Two quivering birches
in the sun
love calls
at dawn
with the fleeting cry of the swallows.

Eyes taken now by life
await the event
delicate maternal hands
cradle the doll.

From what remote regions
have you come
unreal
to these sorrowful shores?
Your existence is a sun
that dazzles:
I feel myself meander
like a river.

Now new torments take hold of me
but sweet ones
that explode in laughter
at times they tighten my throat
with fresh tears
that lead to Paradise.

Alta consolazione è questa
averví
lungo il cammino
amiche.

It’s a deep consolation
having
you as friends along
the road.

Nel sangue odo a notte
fruscio d'ali
uccelli migratori passano e passano
verso approdi d'avventura

Sgomento mi prende nel sonno
e penso ai figli
alle prossime partenze
che faranno solitudine più acuta

I loro giochi di ora conosco
prove e riprove al giorno in cui
salperanno come aironi ai cieli
azzurri del sogno

Il passato lo sconto
in queste ore d'attesa
minuto per minuto
e ha sapore di secoli il travaglio
rivivendo una seconda vita.

At night in my blood I hear
a rustling of wings
migratory birds keep flying past
toward a landfall of adventures

Dismay takes hold of me in sleep
I think about the children
about their coming departures
that will make my isolation more acute

I know their present games
are tests and confirmations for the day
when they sail off like herons for the blue
skies of their dreams

I pay for the past
in these hours of waiting
minute by minute
and travail has the taste of centuries
reliving a second life.

Passeggiata nel bosco

Si va
sbocconcellando un pane
per sentieri obliqui
a un intravisto prato
di smeraldo,
immaginando tesori.

Ad ogni fruscio
volgiamo il capo: che sia
il lupo della fiaba?
Un orso bruno
immigrato?

Gli occhi del bosco
ci spiano innocenti
e irridenti,
costringendoci a una dignità
che non abbiamo in città
anche se il sangue
fa capriole
al frullo improvviso
d'una starna.

Poi, a un tratto, il bosco
allarga le sue braccia
e trovi il prato:
come un altro mondo.

A Walk in the Forest

One goes
nibbling a piece of bread
along roundabout paths
to a once glimpsed emerald
meadow,
imagining treasures.

At every rustle
we turn our heads: is that
the wolf of fairy tales?
An immigrant
brown bear?

The eyes of the forest
watch us, innocent
and mocking,
coercing us to a dignity
we don't have in the city
even though the blood
turns somersaults
at the sudden flapping
of a partridge.

Then, all at once, the forest
spreads its arms
and shows the meadow:
like another world.

Leggo nei tuoi occhi il rimprovero
quando ti ammali
a un padre disarmato al tuo dolore
benché si affanni, purtroppo come un circo,
per darti un sollievo.
E il tuo sorriso mi fa piangere
quando capisci
che la mia vita è tua
e che sono come un muro
sbrecciato da una parte
fra te e la paura.

I read the reproach in your eyes
when you fall ill
of a father powerless against your pain
even though he bustles, sadly like a circus,
to bring you some relief.
And your smile makes me weep
when you realize
that my life is yours
and I am like a wall
breached on one side
between you and fear.

Come pesa la ciminiera
com'è lunga e larga
da casa la vedo
al mattino e alla sera
con il pennacchio da carabiniere
succhia sangue e nafta
come un fungo atomico
mi possiede
e fa grigio il cielo
anche d'estate
al vento e alla pioggia
essa presiede.

How much the smokestack weighs
how high it is and wide
I see it from the house
in the morning and the evening
with its police hat plume
it sucks up blood and diesel
like a mushroom cloud
it possesses me
and it makes the sky gray
even in the summer
in the wind and in the rain
it presides.

Lunedì dopo le ferie

I desideri come topi
hanno divorato
la speranza. I cieli
pallidi ammiccano
alla cronaca nera dei giornali.

Stamane
ci siamo destati al trillo della sveglia
e nel caffè abbiamo rimescolato
con lo zucchero il fruscio nebbioso
dei netturbini, la nevrosi
e il conto della settimana.

Abbiamo sottratto il fatto dal non fatto
il detto dal non detto e constatato
ch'era rimasto ancora un largo spazio
alle trote non pescate
alle mimose non colte
e magari a una stracca dichiarazione
d'amore
per una ragazza passeggera.

Le indecisioni al solito
l'hanno vinta
sulla vita.
Con sorella invidia
al primo muggito di sirena
varchiamo i cancelli della fabbrica

Monday After Vacation

Like mice desires
have devoured
hope. The pallid
skies are winking
at the crime reports in the papers.

This morning
we were wakened by the trill of the alarm clock
and in coffee along with a spoonful of sugar
we stirred the blurred hiss
of streetsweepers, neurosis
and the week's account.

We've subtracted the done from the undone
the said from the unsaid and we've discovered
that there was still a lot of room left over
for the uncaught trout
the unpicked mimosa
and maybe a weary declaration
of love
for a passing girl.

As usual indecisions
have won out
over life.
With sister envy
at the first bellow of the siren
we pass through the factory gates

leggeri come sacchi vuoti
il vuoto macinato da uno dei tanti ritornelli
uditi alla TV.

Tra poco il battito del cuore
sposerà quello della macchina
fino al crepuscolo del giorno.
Sbadiglieremo
sognando la sigaretta
che contrabbandi la voce sopita di Dio.

as light as empty sacks
the emptiness ground up by one of those refrains
heard on TV.

In a bit the beating of the heart
will marry that of the machine
until the twilight of the day.
We'll yawn
dreaming of the cigarette
that smuggles in the dormant voice of God.

Un giorno mi chiuderete gli occhi

alle mie bimbe

Ogni sera
auguratami la buona notte
girate l'interruttore della luce.
Così un giorno mi chiuderete gli occhi.

E più non udrò l'allegro scampanellio
delle vostre voci
non vedrò la folgore del riso
illuminarvi gli occhi
non sentirò il tepore del vostro sonno
scaldarmi il cuore dopo i giuochi
del giorno.

Oh so che dietro la pesante porta
dell'addio troverò il Signore,
ma Egli è come un severo generale
e chissà quanto tempo dovrò stare
sugli attenti
prima che mi conceda il riposo!
E non sarò più il padre che si diletta
coi figli, ma un figlio
che ascolta la predica del Padre
— come un ritorno all'infanzia.
La mia
innocenza allora
vi seguirà come un consiglio
e come il capo della rondine sotto l'ala
fino a quando, adulte, mi darete il volo.

One Day You Will Close My Eyes

to my daughters

Every evening
you wish me a good night
as you turn off the light.
And so one day you will close my eyes.

And I'll no longer hear the merry ring
of your voices
I won't see the lightning of the laughter
illuminate your eyes
I won't feel the radiance of your slumber
warming my heart after
the day's games.

Oh I know that behind the heavy door
of farewell I'll find the Lord,
but He is like a rigid general
and who can say how long I'll have to stand
at attention
before I hear Him say "At ease!"
And I'll no longer be the father who
enjoys his children, but a son
listening to a sermon from his Father
—just like my childhood once again.
And then
my innocence
will follow you like counseling
and like the swallow's head under its wing
until, when you are grown, you fly away.

Così ogni sera
quando girate l'interruttore della luce.

And so it is
every night when you turn off the light.

Notes to the Poems

ISLET OF BERGEGGI

The island of Bergeggi, roughly twenty acres in area, lies in the Ligurian Sea near the village of Bergeggi, in northwestern Italy. It contains the remains of a fourth-century church and a tenth-century monastery.

Contini may have had the Northern Irish songwriter Jimmy Kennedy (1902–1984) in mind. Principally a lyricist, not a composer, Kennedy wrote the words to "Red Sails in the Sunset," "The Isle of Capri," "South of the Border," "The Teddy Bears' Picnic," and hundreds of other songs.

Andantino mosso is a term of musical notation that signifies movement a little faster than a walking pace.

A FOREST IN THE DARK IS YOUR BECOMING

Armand Godoy (1880–1964) was a Cuban Symbolist poet who wrote principally in French. Born in Havana and raised in Lima, he worked in finance with the intention of becoming wealthy enough to live in Paris and devote himself to literature, a goal he achieved by the age of forty.

BENGAL LIGHTS AT MY WEDDING

Bengal lights are bright bluish-white flares, often used for signaling at sea. The name is believed to come from the fact that Bengal was a principal source of saltpeter, one of the main ingredients of the lights.

TWO POEMS FOR P. (1950)

Harry Lime is the character played by Orson Welles in Carol Reed's 1949 film *The Third Man*. The title music from the film's soundtrack, written and performed on zither by Anton Karas, was variously released under the titles "The Third Man Theme" and "The Harry Lime Theme." There was also a vocal version performed by Don Cherry, with lyrics by Walter Lord, author of *A Night to Remember*.

THAT THE GOOD TRADE WIND . . .

Tiresia dixit is Latin for "Tiresias said." Tiresias's story appears in Ovid's *Metamorphoses*, Book III. Transformed to a woman for striking a pair of copulating snakes, he struck them again seven years later and regained his manly form. Called to settle a quarrel between Zeus and Hera, he agreed with Zeus that women enjoyed the sexual act more than women (ten times as much, in his informed view); in anger, Hera struck him blind, for which Zeus compensated him with the gift of second sight, or prophecy. Tiresias appears prominently in Sophocles' *Oedipus the King* and pivotally in T. S. Eliot's *The Waste Land.*

DICEBANT MIHI SODALES . . .

The phrase *Dicebant mihi sodales* . . . is the beginning of a Latin distich, "*Dicebant mihi sodales, si sepulchrum amicae visitarem, / curas meas aliquantulum forelevatas*" ("My companions told me that visiting the grave of my beloved might ease my misery a little"). Written by Ebn Zaiat, a poet who flourished in Baghdad in the early third century, the couplet achieved wide circulation as the epigraph to Edgar Allan Poe's tale "Berenice" (1835). Poe's source for the Latin text is the *Bibliotèque Orientale* (1697) of Barthélemy d'Herbelot de Molainville (1625–1695).

Édith Piaf (1915–1963) was a well-known French cabaret singer and songwriter, whose most popular songs include *La Vie en rose* and *Non, je ne regrette rien.*

CITY

Quidquid latet, apparebit is a phrase from the medieval Latin hymn *Dies Irae* ("Day of Wrath"). Its sixth stanza reads: "*Judex ergo cum sedebit, / Quidquid latet apparebit: / Nil inultum remanebit*" ("Therefore, when the judge takes his seat, that which is hidden will be revealed: Nothing will remain unpunished").

THE RIVER

Gherardo del Colle (1920–1978) was an Italian poet and Capuchin friar.

The Twilight

Et alors je pense à ton Désir: Contini's note to this poem cites (in Italian translation) the following passages from *Les Nourritures Terrestres* (*The Fruits of the Earth*, 1897) by French novelist and diarist Andre Gide (1869–1951): "It was necessary, for a certain time, to consent to the denial of all morality and to no longer resist any desires. They alone were able to educate me. I surrendered." "Then, later . . . No, it was neither decrease of desires nor surfeit that I felt coming with the years; but often, expiating on my greedy lips the too swift depletion of pleasure, possession seemed to me of less value than pursuit, and I came increasingly to prefer thirst to fulfillment, the promise of delight to the thing itself, the endless swelling of love to satisfaction."

THE ROADS

Joseph Joubert (1754–1824) wrote essays and aphorisms throughout his life, but published nothing. *Recueil des pensées de M. Joubert* appeared posthumously in 1838. Other, more complete editions of Joubert's writings have since been published. "*Le corps est la baraque où notre existence est campée*" translates to "The body is the house where our existence is encamped."

Beaux gars, beaux gars! is French for "Handsome lads, handsome lads!"

Mon pays est Paris: "My country is Paris"; the phrase is a virtual homonym of a line in *J'ai deux amours*, a cabaret song introduced by Josephine Baker in 1930: "*J'ai deux amours, / Mon pays et paris*" ("I have two loves, my country and Paris").

La chair est triste, hélas! is the beginning of Stéphane Mallarmé's poem *Brise Marine* ("Sea Breeze," 1864): "*La chair est triste, hélas! et j'ai lu tous les livres*" ("The flesh is sad, alas!, and I have read all the books").

A trois heures / le sang bouillonne: "At three o'clock the blood boils" (French).

A GIFT TOO DEAR

Angelo Barile (1888–1967) was an Italian poet. His correspondence with his fellow Ligurian Gherardo del Colle was published in 2012.

PAPER FLOWER

Tristan Derème (pseudonym of Philippe Huc, 1889–1941), was a French Surrealist poet. Section CXL of his book-length poem *La Verdure dorée* (The Golden Greenery, 1922) contains the following passage: "*Tu n'es plus là. J'ai lu Delille et l'Annuaire / Des Téléphones, pour ne plus songer à tes / Sanglots; mais je voyais tes larmes et restais / Des heures, les yeux clos. . . .*" ("You're no longer here. I've read Delille and the telephone book, to keep from thinking about your sobs; but I saw your tears and remained for hours, eyes closed. . . .").

Luc Durtain (pseudonym of André Nepveu, 1881–1959) was a French poet, novelist, and physician. "*Nuit. Silence. O fin de chaque jour* . . ." translates to "Night. Silence. O the end of every day . . ."

Hidalgo is a Spanish term signifying a gentleman or a member of the nobility. The full title of Cervantes' classic novel is *El ingenioso hidalgo don Quijote de la Mancha*.

Ite, missa est ("Go, the mass is ended") is spoken at the conclusion of the Latin mass.

sicut comoedians: *sicut* is Latin for *as*; *comoedians* is an early English form of *comedians*, derived from the Latin *coemedius*.

THE SONG OF HOPE

Jean-Marie Domenach (1922–1997) was a French editor, professor, and intellectual of Catholic leftist sympathies. "*Les héros de demain sont les emprisonnés d'aujourd'hui*" means "Tomorrow's heroes are today's prisoners."

Pier delle Vigne (1190–1249) was an Italian diplomat and secretary to Emperor Frederick II of the Holy Roman Empire. Denounced and imprisoned on false charges, he committed suicide in his cell. He makes a notable appearance in Canto XIII of Dante's *Inferno*.

The hill on which Jesus Christ was crucified is known as Golgotha, the Place of the Skull.

SARDINIA

The Nuragic civilization flourished on Sardinia for nearly two millennia beginning around 1800 BC. Some 7000 of its megalithic structures, known as nuraghes, remain on the island.

YOUR FACE IS A BLANK AMAZEMENT IN THIS DAWN

Contini wrote the following note on the manuscript of this poem: "Everything hinges on this: 'death discounts living' and it is made from the despair of man who comes into the world unwillingly and is only a thing that the days hurl into the light of life and through all of the passions for this: he suddenly finds himself before the ultimate night. He is born with a blank amazement and he ends up with all the burdens of an entire existence in the evening."

O BABYLON

In marble architecture, a caryatid is a draped female figure functioning as a column or pillar to support an entablature.

WOMAN AND SPRINGTIME

"I don't know where I was born / but I'm certain Maremma didn't undo me": this passage alludes to the famous line in Canto V of Dante's *Purgatorio*, "*Siena mi fé, disfecemi Maremma*" ("Siena made me, Maremma unmade me"). The speaker is Pia, customarily associated with Pia de' Tolomei, who was believed to have been murdered by her husband.

ON THE YELLOW BACKDROP OF POZZOLANA

Pozzolana is a porous variety of volcanic ash used to make hydraulic cement.

EVENING MASS

Paphos is a city in southwestern Cyprus. In classical times it was the capital, and was visited by the Apostle Paul.

In music, a diesis is a quarter tone.

WHEN I MET UP WITH YOU, O SILENUS

In mythology, Silenus was the mentor and companion of Dionysus, the Greek god of wine. He was older than the satyrs and had the characteristics of a horse, not a goat. In *The Birth of Tragedy*, Friedrich Nietzsche tells how King Midas sought Silenus to ask him what is best or most desirable in a man's life. Silenus responded that the best thing is to have never been born, not to exist, to be nothing. Failing that, the best thing is to die soon (see Philip Larkin's "This Be the Verse": "Get out as early as you can").

The Tirso is the principal river of Sardinia.

O YOU, YOUNG GIRLS WHO GO OUT ON THE BEACH

Tiresias: see note to "That the Good Trade Wind" above.

ONE DAY IN NOVEMBER

At the beginning of the Latin mass, the priest intones "*Introibo ad altare Dei*" ("I will go in unto the altar of God"), to which the server responds "*Ad Deum qui laetificat juventutem meam*" ("To God who gives joy to my youth"). Contini's formulation, *laetificabat*, changes the predicate to the past tense: "gave joy."

In the sixth century B.C., King Nebuchadnezzar II undertook extensive reconstruction of Babylon, then the largest city in the world. His projects included a system of massive defensive walls, much of which still stands, encircling the city.

ALAS, LORD, I'M TIRED OF FIGHTING AGAINST HYPOCRISY

In the Calypso episode of James Joyce's *Ulysses*, the novel's fourth section, the protagonist Leopold Bloom is introduced. Among his other morning activities, he pays a visit to the outhouse, where he reads a prize story in a popular magazine while defecating.

Acknowledgments

"Lord, the Wall Has Risen," "The Song of Hope," and "And You Won't Live . . ." were published in *A Life Gambled in Poetry: Homage to Alfredo de Palchi*, edited by Luigi Fontanella (Gradiva, 2011). I am deeply grateful to Graziella Sidoli and Antonello Borra, each of whom read the entire manuscript with scrupulous sympathy and offered a number of extremely valuable suggestions. I thank Francesca Bergadano for permission to translate her comprehensive essay on Contini's life and work, for her judicious editing and selection of the poems that make up this volume, and for all her efforts to secure for Contini's work the attention and respect that it deserves. As always, I am indebted to Lisa Cicchetti and Areta Buk for their artistry in producing so handsome a volume, inside and out. And, as always, I owe a great deal to Alfredo de Palchi for inspiring and encouraging this project, and for introducing me to a fine and often fascinating poet whom I would never have otherwise discovered.

About the Author

ENNIO CONTINI was born in Oristano, on the island of Sardinia, on May 31, 1914. When he was very young, his family moved to Savona, in the coastal province of Liguria in northwestern Italy, and Liguria remained his home for the rest of his long life. During the late 1930s he began to publish literary and cultural essays in nationally prominent periodicals, and his first book of poetry, *Magnolia*, appeared in 1939. An officer in the Italian army during the Second World War, Contini was wounded in battle. At the end of the war he was tried for actions relating to his military service and condemned to death, a sentence that was later commuted to life imprisonment. Ultimately, he served nine years in the prisons of Savona, Procida, and Civitavecchia. In 1952 Contini published *L'Alleluja*, poems largely based on his prison experiences, in a volume that also contained the first ten of Ezra Pound's *Cantos* in an Italian translation by Pound's daughter, Mary de Rachewiltz. Contini's later publications were the poetry collections *Schegge d'anima* (1962) and *Viaggio nel buio* (1969) and a novel, *No haya cuartel!* (1995). Severely incapacitated after a stroke, he died on November 14, 2006.

About the Editor

FRANCESCA BERGADANO studied modern and contemporary Italian literature at the University of Pisa, writing her thesis on the relationship between Louis-Ferdinand Céline and Surrealism; her essay on this subject can be read at lf-celine.blogspot.com. She completed her studies at the University of Genoa with a thesis on the Italian Futurist poet Vittorio Osvaldo Tommasini, who published under the name of Farfa. She is currently pursuing her doctoral research there with a concentration on Ennio Contini, whose personal archive she has studied and organized. With her thorough grounding in Contini's life and work and the full cooperation of his family, she is uniquely qualified to edit and introduce his poetry.

About the Translator

MICHAEL PALMA's poetry volumes are *The Egg Shape*, *Antibodies*, *A Fortune in Gold*, *Begin in Gladness*, and an online chapbook, *The Ghost of Congress Street*. His sixteen previous translations of Italian poets include prize-winning volumes of Guido Gozzano and Diego Valeri and a fully rhymed translation of Dante's *Inferno*, as well as two earlier volumes with Chelsea Editions: Maurizio Cucchi's *No Part to Play: Selected Poems 1965–2009*, and Giovanni Raboni's *Every Third Thought: Selected Poems 1950–2004*. His most recent books are a translation from Paolo Valesio, *Il servo rosso / The Red Servant: Selected Poems 1979–2002* (with Graziella Sidoli), and *Faithful in My Fashion: Essays on the Translation of Poetry*.